To Reign or N

To Reign or Not to Reign

John Knight

The Pentland Press Limited
Edinburgh • Cambridge • Durham • USA

© John Knight 2000

First published in 2000 by
The Pentland Press Ltd.
1 Hutton Close
South Church
Bishop Auckland
Durham

All rights reserved.
Unauthorised duplication
contravenes existing laws.

British Library Cataloguing in Publication Data.
A Catalogue record for this book is available
from the British Library.

ISBN 1 85821 823 3

Typeset by CBS, Martlesham Heath, Ipswich, Suffolk
Printed and bound by Antony Rowe Ltd., Chippenham

CONTENTS

1.	To Reign or Not to Reign?	1
2.	The Wilderness Experience	9
3.	Doubt and Unbelief	21
4.	Resurrection Power?	27
5.	Resurrection: Fact or Fantasy?	41
6.	Martyrs and Tyrants	57
7.	Panic Attacks	63
8.	God's Promises Fulfilled	71
9.	Team Spirit: Growth or Compromise?	77
10.	Productive Confrontation	87
11.	What Dreams are Made of	99
12.	Tell It Like It Is	113
13.	Who is this Jesus?	133
14.	Parable of the Eagle	143
15.	Not Retired – Re-fired!	159
16.	New Wine from Old Skins	171
17.	The Challenge of the Familiar	185
18.	The Proof of the Pudding . . . or Ask Tracy	197
19.	Clinging to a Lamppost at Dawn!	211
	Epilogue	225

PREFACE

Billy Graham said 'no alcoholic was ever more in bondage to his habit of drink than many Christians are to their habit of doubting. In fact, many Christians have settled down under their doubts as though they had contracted an incurable disease'.

We cannot but be unaware of the levels of doubt and unbelief amongst Christians – especially, surprisingly, those in leadership. Basic doctrines of faith and Biblical credibility are not only questioned, but actually denied. So is it surprising that many in our 'pick and mix' society, given such questionable leadership, believe anything or nothing?

To Reign or Not to Reign is an attempt to provide a positive response to these issues.

Fourteen years ago, at the age of fifty, my family and I were forced to leave our homeland Zimbabwe, and start life again in a new country. During that first year, while looking for work, I wrote *Rain in a Dry Land*. Michael Cassidy described it as a 'veritable twentieth century Acts of the Spirit' with 'mind-boggling evidences of God's supernatural workings and protection . . . in the 'Rhodesian' guerilla war' and 'incontrovertible evidence of a God who is alive and well and on the job in our tattered 20th Century world'. It also dealt with personal life-changing experiences – discovering a God who is very much alive and active – after spending the first fifteen years of my ministry as a rather reluctant priest.

So many have asked, mainly because they have no personal or congregational experience of God doing great exploits: Do these things only happen in the third world? The answer clearly is 'no'!

Soon after coming to Greens Norton I was asked to speak at a Mothers Union meeting in a village near here. A lady who was virtually stone deaf asked for prayer. God wonderfully restored her hearing, and this brought such blessings to her and her family in the last year of her life. *To Reign or Not to Reign*, as a sequel to *Rain in a Dry Land*, tells of a God who is just as wonderfully at work in this country. In it I share many testimonies to His healing love and grace, both in our own lives and in the lives of so many others.

Faith makes things possible – it does not make them easy. *(Anon)*

John Knight
22nd July, 2000
Greens Norton

> All quotations, unless otherwise stated, are from the *Good News Bible*. The author's emphases are in italics.
>
> A number of names have been changed to protect the identity of some whose stories have been told.

'What is faith? It is the confident assurance that what we hope for is going to happen. It is the evidence of things we cannot see.'

> Hebrews. 11:1 New Living Translation

Copies of the author's previous book, Rain in a Dry Land, priced £3.00 each (inclusive of postage and packaging) are available from:

The Revd. J.F.A.M. Knight
The Rectory
Towcester Road
Greens Norton
Northamptonshire
NN12 8BL
England

Chapter 1

TO REIGN OR NOT TO REIGN?

'God moves in mysterious ways His wonders to perform'! That was certainly true of one of our daughter's Sports Days. Most young children are excited on such an occasion; seven-year-old Lynne and her school friends were no exception. However, when we arrived at the school, with the field beautifully marked and laid out for the event, it was to find enormous black clouds directly overhead. And if that was not enough, there was an even more ominous gathering of storm clouds over to the west, with a wind blowing so strongly in our direction that the willows in the field below us were bent almost double.

Lynne's school was a church school. No suggestion was made that the problem be committed to prayer. And I suppose that if the organisers had stopped everything and called on everyone to pray for clear skies, there would have been surprise and general embarrassment all round. Laughter, too, perhaps. The problem would not necessarily be with the children (many have a wonderfully simple faith in God!); it would have been the adults. You can picture the scene for yourself. As rain drops begin to fall, the announcer calls on the crowd to join with him in prayer for clear skies . . . ?

No! Rather, because so few expect God to work in that way (or, possibly, are too frightened to lay their faith on the line in case such specific prayer isn't answered) what we in fact heard was a very different announcement over the loud hailer. 'You can see from the coming storm that we will not get through the programme. So we intend to rush through as many events as possible before the storm breaks!' The proposal was clearly accepted as perfectly reasonable. It was certainly one that was in line with most people's perceived acceptance that nothing could be done to alter 'those facts'.

Three of us, sitting together amongst that large gathering of parents, often prayed together. So I said to my wife Jill and our friend Janie, 'Let's ask God for clear skies right now.' I thought I had spoken fairly quietly, but a lady sitting next to me overheard my suggestion and chipped in: 'I gave up praying for that sort of thing years ago; it never works!'

For our part, I told her, our experience in Africa had shown us a God who actually delights in answering prayer. We believed in the power of prayer; so we would pray in faith for the miracle needed to enable the children to enjoy the afternoon. Nothing ventured, nothing gained!

After two or three minutes the rain drops from the heavy clouds over us stopped. A short while later I looked up and saw that the willow trees were now bent over in the opposite direction! The clouds above us, and the storm following, moved off in that direction. A moment or two later the sky cleared, and the remainder of the sports afternoon was bathed in warm sunshine. All the events on the programme were completed. Then, as the last presentation was made, the clouds returned, this time we had to run for cover. Most of us were drenched! But the children's joy was complete. 'To God be the glory, great things He has done!'

Should it really surprise us that God cares for us on a personal level? No one was deprived of rain; only the timing was altered. Such incidents have become known. When good weather is essential for special events (like Diocesan events at Lamport Hall, or church summer fêtes) people have asked us to pray for good weather and been thrilled (indeed amazed) at having rain-free, or beautiful sunny, or even wonderfully hot, days for those events. Should such things surprise us?

'The British Isles gets the weather the people deserve'! Could that be true? None can be unaware of how pessimistic, even downright negative, the majority of the people of Britain are when discussing the weather! When a special event is planned, we often hear such comments as: 'It's always cold and miserable then!' Or, 'What will we do if it rains? Where will we then hold the event?'

Someone will be sure to cap that comment with one of those sweeping generalisations heard when the weather is discussed: 'We no longer have the long hot summers we had when I was a child . . .' The reverse is equally true. If better than average weather is experienced, people say, 'It won't last'; or, 'You mark my words, we will pay for this!' and prophesy doom and gloom as a result.

It's true, isn't it? Few people act as if they believe anything can be done to alter the weather. Certainly few believe it seems to me, that prayer (and therefore God) can change it.

How short people's memories are! The British nation was called to prayer when their army had been driven back at Dunkirk by Hitler's lightning invasion of the Low Countries. With no escape, and their backs to the sea, the whole nation prayed for those men. And then, do you remember what followed? Against all the odds, the Channel was 'as smooth as a millpond' and the smallest of boats made it across to help in the dramatic rescue of the British Task Force. Without the miracle – and most accepted it *was* a miracle – the losses would have been appalling. Against all the odds, the great majority returned to fight another day.

Where is that faith in prayer, in a God who is able, in Britain today? The Scriptures challenge us about this state of affairs, and about the negative and unbelieving attitudes we so often adopt – often without being aware of what we are doing!

Look at something the Bible teaches. The psalmist reminds us of the close, individual and personal relationship God has with each one of us:

> You made all the delicate inner parts of my body, and knit them together in my mother's womb. Thank You for making me so wonderfully complex! It is amazing to think about. Your workmanship is marvellous – and how well I know it. You were

there while I was being formed in utter seclusion! You saw me before I was born and scheduled each day of my life before I began to breathe [something the pro-abortionist lobby needs to consider?] How precious it is, Lord, to realise that You are thinking about me constantly! I can't even count how many times a day Your thoughts turn towards me. And when I waken in the morning, You are still thinking of me . . . !'[1]

If God is so intimately involved with every moment of our lives then surely He is willing, where it is right, to bring about change – in even the smallest detail – in the lives of those He loves? Yet despite the truth of all this, the tendency is to laugh it all off. We believe, simply by failing to do anything, that there is nothing we can do to change the circumstances surrounding our lives – be it the weather, or a headache, or whatever. Be honest! Are you, if only occasionally, negative or pessimistic about such things? It is certainly often true of me, particularly at times when my faith level plummets for one reason or another! If *your* answer is 'yes', you too may have a spiritual problem. Think about it . . .

It has to do, for want of a better description, with what one might label as a 'mindset'. Some people seem to be critical of everyone and everything. Criticism becomes such a habit that eventually the person is oblivious to what he or she is doing and becomes a 'pain in the neck'. It is avoidable because, in part at least, it results from the person's on-going negative, unforgiving, (yes, sometimes even hateful) attitude towards an individual or individuals; or is brought about by events or circumstances connected with that person's life. Now the same kind of mindset can apply to our attitude to the weather. Just as we have to do something positive to deal with a critical or carping spirit, so we need to be positive over attitudes about the weather; to put a guard on our lips; to say nothing unless we have something positive to say. But there is still more to it than that.

Once we become negative and critical about the weather (or anything else for that matter), that critical or negative attitude doesn't stop there.

It insidiously begins to permeate, as a mindset, every other area of our lives. It might be our daily complaints about government, the hole in the ozone layer, the Church, the vicar, a member of the family or erstwhile friend, our anger over straitened circumstances, or about any number of issues. If you find that difficult to believe, spend a little time observing the faces, the words used – and the spirit in which they are said – of those involved, for instance, in present-day politics, or those involved in television interviews.

And it goes much deeper than that. Jonathan Miller wrote:

> Nowhere else is the cult of misery so entrenched and nowhere else is so much pleasure taken in a zeitgeist of gloom. The British are not merely miserable, they are brilliant at it . . . it cannot be coincidental that two of the biggest television hits, *One Foot in the Grave* and *Inspector Morse*, both revolve around characters who have elevated woe to an art form. [He concludes] If we can be conditioned to misery, why can we not condition ourselves to take a more balanced view: to exalt in achievement, rejoice in success and value those things about Britain which remain good . . . ? In his article Miller quotes Laurie Taylor – professor of sociology at York – who says, 'It's all part of what Norman Tebbit called the culture of negativism. We've turned grumbling into an art form.'[2]

If that negative or critical spirit in an individual is not checked, the subject eventually becomes so embittered that he loses friends, and much else besides. So we know it is important to lovingly show the person what he is doing to himself. Then it's up to the subject to start changing that mindset – not only by biting his tongue every time he is about to say something critical, but by thinking of something good, positive or complimentary to say in its place!

Surely the most important thing of all is to see that a negative mindset *effectively denies God's control or ability to bring about change* – whether it be in respect of a person, situation or circumstance. Let me repeat that. Intended or not, we effectively deny God's ability to bring about change. Now you and I can only change that mindset when we acknowledge that there is nothing *we* can do about it; *but God can*! When we positively turn that person or situation over to God, we ask God to bring about whatever is needed.

Before reaching that stage, however, we have to ask ourselves the question: 'Do we actually believe God *can* bring about such change, or *perform* such signs?' And because that faith level can be so mercurial, we have to review the question continually. It reminds us to look to God, not to ourselves, to bring about whatever is needed.

It is very important to note that this has nothing to do with the power of positive thinking, nor has it anything to do with auto-suggestion. It has *everything* to do with the acceptance of, and belief in, God's promises to us as contained in Scripture, and that with Him 'nothing is impossible'.[3]

'Oh yes! God can do signs and wonders, or work miracles,' we may be willing to admit. Yet, isn't it true, that the areas in which we have the greatest difficulty concerning them is when it has to do with just the ordinary, everyday things – like the weather, or a cold, or a headache, or regular monthly menstrual pain or PMT? Some find it easier to think of God getting involved in such miracles as 'walking on water' or 'raising the dead'.

'Stop your doubting and believe',[4] Jesus said to Thomas. On another occasion He said to his disciples: 'Ask' [literally 'go on and on and on asking', the original Greek implies] 'and you *will* receive'.[5] James, one of the disciples, wrote: 'you do not have, because you do not ask'.[6]

It's easy to illustrate why doubt and unbelief can have such a crippling effect. It's important to recognise the mercurial nature of our believing and doubting. Our human nature being what it is, we find ourselves – if we recognise the syndrome – waging an almost constant battle with those negative attitudes that so easily rise to the surface. No sooner do we think we have got our act together – and we really begin to believe in, and trust, God to undertake – than a new set of circumstances presents itself. In a flash our doubts, and consequent failure to trust God for the solution, take control of us once more.

Probably one of the most dramatic illustrations of this – with equally devastating consequences – is the story of the people of Israel standing with Moses on the threshold of the Promised Land. Of all people, they really had no excuse for what was to follow.

NOTES:
[1] Psalm 139:13–18 (*Living Bible*)
[2] News Review, *Sunday Times* 13 June, 1993. Page 6. Article entitled 'Cheer Up, Britain – It's not as bad as you think' by Jonathan Miller.
[3] Mark 10:27
[4] John 20:27b
[5] Luke 11:9
[6] James 4:2b (*RSV*)

Chapter 2

THE WILDERNESS EXPERIENCE

These Jews had witnessed a whole series of events of almost mind-blowing proportions in the months before their escape from Egypt. The late twentieth century overturning of communist regimes, pulling down of the Berlin Wall and 'freeing' of eastern bloc countries – especially Romania from its megalomaniac tyrant Ceaucescu in late 1989 – come close to it! The Jews' escape from Egypt was followed by the truly miraculous crossing of the Red Sea and the destruction of Pharaoh's pursuing army. Those events (surely?) gave them plenty of proof of God's trustworthiness, and His ability to do the impossible.

Yet, what incredibly short memories these people had! Only a few weeks later twelve spies were sent in to the Promised Land. It did not take them long to forget what God could do; faced with the humanly impossible odds involved in the conquest of the land, God no longer registered in the equation. Anxiety and fear, doubt and unbelief, a mindset, took control. The real issue came down to this: miracles for others may be all right. But the real test for ten of those spies, as it is for us, was this: 'Would God consider carrying out a miracle just for . . . me?'

That, basically, is the great hurdle each has to surmount; not just once, but every time we experience a new challenge. On this occasion, only two of the twelve spies had the faith to believe.

Those two men, Joshua and Caleb, believed the Jews *could* conquer the land, but not through any particular ability of the Jews. It was God who would work that miracle for them. Unlike the other ten, they *did* bring God into their calculations: 'Do not rebel against the Lord and don't be afraid of the people who live there' [they said]. 'We will conquer them easily'. [How?] 'The Lord is with us . . .'[1] they affirmed.

Who says a majority vote is always the right one? How many times do we get it wrong because we act on that assumption in our synods, committees, and councils? Because the majority vote carried the day and they failed to trust God, none of their generation (apart from Joshua and Caleb – the ones with faith to believe) would ever see the Promised Land. The 'majority' sentenced the whole nation to forty years in the wilderness! During that time they would learn anew the lessons they should have learnt from earlier experiences. How like us!

The desert was not to prove a comfortable classroom. But there were compensations. Despite their unbelief, God continued to demonstrate His love and power in providing for every need – miraculously. Look at the evidence.

Would anyone enjoy an existence without a permanent home, constantly on the move but always within the confines of the desert? Think of the consequences for those Jews. Every time one was nicely settled with a fixed routine, with everything in its right place, the cloud or pillar of fire would move on. Moses would cry out, 'Let God arise, let His enemies be scattered!'[2] And whether you liked it or not you, with everyone else, would pack up and have to move with the cloud or fiery pillar. Most carried more than their own possessions. Why? Because a large body of men had to carry the tabernacle and all that went with it. Further, small children and the elderly would be unable to carry their fair share. So the rest would have carried more.

You would never have been free of sand; in your hair, your clothes, your bedding, your food; in your ears, eyes, mouth and nose. It reminds me of the humorous and poignant addition to the well-known chorus 'Give me oil in my lamp, keep me burning': 'Give me sand in my shoes, keep me humble'! They would certainly have experienced that! But had they known the song, would they have cheerfully joined in the refrain: 'Sing hosanna! sing hosanna! sing hosanna to the King of kings'

The Wilderness Experience

...? I think not. The Biblical record shows they did a lot of complaining!

The desert was to be a place of learning. The lessons were very simple: firstly, the need for absolute obedience to God, and secondly, the need for a faith which enables one to move beyond what is humanly possible, into the supernatural realm – even for little 'me'! A case of trusting not in ourselves, but in God: learning to deal with doubt and unbelief, and acknowledging and drawing upon God's supernatural power, for everything.

Perhaps it would be an encouragement to us to know that even the spiritual giants frequently fail this test. Consider Moses. Despite all the miracles witnessed before they camped at Kadesh, he too failed when challenged to take yet another step of faith. Let me explain what happened.

Until that moment, Moses had been privy to a secret unknown to the Jews he brought from Egypt. Moses spent forty years in the wilderness herding his father-in-law's sheep before receiving his present commission. The secret he had learnt was this. In the desert, rainwater is rapidly stored in the rock. A chemical reaction takes place sealing the water within. A little local knowledge reveals where water may be found once you locate and strike one of those 'chemical seals' hard enough. Break it, and water is released. So when Moses had struck the rock with his stick on an earlier occasion, he was hailed as a miracle worker! And he was, to the extent that he found water when the people thought they were dying of thirst. But now comes the crunch...

Instead of striking the rock with his stick this time, God orders Moses to *speak* to (NOT strike) the rock to make it give up its water.[3] *That* is at the heart of what we need to hear. A level of faith is needed to believe God can and will do miraculously what, humanly speaking, we are unable to do in the natural realm.

Now Moses just couldn't bring himself to believe and trust God at that point. Amongst other things, it was bound up with a possible loss of face. A problem familiar to church leaders?

Moses had been there before. They had faced certain defeat when they had their backs to the Red Sea, with Pharaoh's armies almost on top of them. As Moses turned to God for help, God told him to raise his stick over the water and the waters would part. Would you have believed it possible if you had been in his shoes? Well, surprise, surprise, Moses also had problems! He immediately went back to prayer. Exasperated, God asked him why he continued to cry out for help. The way the Living Bible puts it so delightfully is: 'Quit praying, and get moving!'[4] I've already told you what to do – just do it! Easier said than done! But when Moses obeyed, it worked!

Returning to the water supply problem, God now tells Moses to '*speak* to that rock'.[5] Of course, there is always the element of doubt as to whether we have heard God aright in those situations, isn't there? If Moses did what he was told, and nothing happened, he would lose face in front of all those people. How much easier, then, to do something that he knew wouldn't fail: use his natural human wit and *strike* the rock, rather than 'speak' to it.

As with the ten unbelieving spies, Moses' lack of trust in God resulted in him losing his chance to enter the Promised Land. 'The Lord reprimanded Moses and Aaron. He said, "Because you did not have enough faith to acknowledge My holy power before the people of Israel, you will not lead them into the land that I promised to give them."'[6]

How harsh that judgement appears to us. How many of us would have failed that test? How many other 'tests' do we fail? Think of those many occasions we thought we could do nothing about the weather, or an illness, or a headache, or whatever. And for those of us who are church leaders there is an added dimension. If, as a result of our own lack of faith we fail to 'acknowledge [God's] holy power before the people',[7] we fail the people we serve!

Removing all the miracles from the Exodus story would leave us with a story no one would have bothered to record. As it is, the evidence reveals an extraordinary God of the Universe – a God who loves, cares, trains and disciplines, so that a faith-filled, believing people are able to experience all that the Living God can accomplish on their behalf. Fortunately for us, Exodus faithfully records the signs and wonders performed by this Living God.

The Wilderness Experience

Those Jews in the time of Exodus experienced the world's first ever air-conditioning unit (the cloud by day performing that function) and the world's first central heating system (the pillar of fire by night)! How essential in an environment where temperatures can exceed 40 degrees centigrade in the day, but also get very cold at night. They had to move whenever the cloud or pillar of fire moved. This in itself was a reminder of God's divine guidance day by day; and important when one considers the pollution caused by a large body of people[8] and their livestock in one small area around the camp for any length of time. No doubt there were times when people objected to moving! Perhaps a Mum dug her heels in because she was fed up with packing and unpacking. If she and her family decided to stay and not follow the others, the family would very soon discover the consequences. Not only the loss of the air-conditioning and heating 'units', but the loss of their food and water supplies as well! Fortunately, because a caring God was in control of the move, the pace of the move was such that even the smallest and weakest members could keep up. So anyone left behind of their own freewill would soon catch up and enjoy once more the creature comforts God provided.

I would soon have tired of the unchanging diet. There couldn't have been too many ways, with or without other ingredients, of preparing or cooking quails and 'manna' (the Hebrew word 'manna' literally means 'What is it?'). There were no supermarket chains or entrepreneurs to bring in supplies from outside the desert. Yet their clothes and shoes did not wear out during those forty years![9] When one carries everything one possesses, from tents to small children, no one would have had too many changes of clothing. The fashion-conscious amongst them would not have appreciated that.

But over the forty-year period they learnt the two lessons: that obedience to God pays off; and that when all human resources fail, not only is our God able to supply our every need (note 'need' as opposed to desire or want), He actually enjoys taking up the challenge when we move from the realm of the possible to the impossible, thereby delighting those who trust and believe in Him.

We discover how well the Jews had learnt those lessons when they stood on the edge of the Jordan prior to making another bid to enter the Promised Land. The river was in full flood. No way was it fordable! Joshua had, on the death of Moses, been appointed leader of the Jews. God had promised him: 'I will always be with you; I will never abandon you.'[10] God's commissioning of Joshua included a thrice-repeated injunction: 'Be determined and confident!'[11] Seldom is something repeated three times in Scripture, but when it is, it is always significant.

Before entering the Promised Land, the Jews were 'tested' once more. The purpose of it was to see if they had learnt from their experience in the wilderness. 'When you see the priests carrying the Covenant Box of the Lord your God, break camp and follow them . . . purify yourselves, because tomorrow the Lord will perform miracles among you'. Then on the following day . . . 'When the priests who carry the Covenant Box of the Lord of all the earth put their feet in the water, the Jordan will stop flowing, and the water coming downstream will pile up . . .'[12]

This time there was no hesitation. Their faith was honoured, for as they stepped into the raging torrent, 'the flow downstream to the Dead Sea was completely cut off, and the people were able to cross over. The people walked across on dry ground, the priests carrying the Lord's Covenant Box stood on dry ground in the middle of the Jordan until all the people had crossed over.'[13]

A lesson learnt. But, such being the perversity of God's people, soon to be forgotten. They tried to capture Ai in their own strength – the result of the euphoria after the capture of Jericho – and failed! Then the lesson had to be painfully re-learnt, only to be forgotten again, with the cycle repeated over and over again down through the centuries. This is a lesson most of us timid twenty-first century church members, sad to say, have still to discover and learn for ourselves.

It is at this level that our liberal theologians, for example, have difficulty. They cannot accept God can override the natural laws of science. So, for them, some important Church doctrines, although clearly stated in Scripture and held to be true by Christians for twenty centuries, have (in their understanding) to be altered or abandoned – including the miraculous conception, the Virgin Birth, Jesus' bodily Resurrection and Ascension, His Second Coming, and so on.

Further, miracles in the Old Testament as well as the miracles of Jesus and the New Testament Church – if these modern theologians are right – are to be discarded or re-interpreted without reference to 'a miraculous element'. Miracles like changing water into wine, walking on the water, feeding the four/five thousand, endless healings, raising the dead – anything, in fact, which speaks of a 'God-intervention'! In *their* estimation, miracles are unacceptable at face value because God does not interfere with, or transgress, the laws He has set. Is it any wonder that doubt and unbelief are rife?

'Scholarly' unbelief is a crucial issue to be faced. If we were to accept the arguments of liberal theologians, then much that is written throughout the Bible would have to be discounted. No wonder a cartoon in a national newspaper pictured sidesmen handing out a tiny slip of paper to worshippers entering Durham Cathedral with the caption: 'We haven't dispensed with the Bible completely, but this is the bit the Bishop actually believes to be true'.[14]

Another theologian, whose otherwise superb commentaries are read and studied by thousands, does have one major shortcoming. He is unable to accept miracles. So, for instance, he explains the 'feeding of the five thousand' something like this: Everyone had actually taken their sandwiches along with them in their handbags or hip pockets! And though Jesus challenged them with the problem of how everyone might be fed, only the little boy was willing to share his lunch box with them. The rest were then so ashamed of their selfishness that they too pulled out their sandwiches – and as with every church 'Bring and Share' meal – there was enough food left over to fill twelve baskets with the remains! He doesn't explain where the twelve baskets came from. Another embarrassment perhaps? Had the disciples gone away quietly and eaten their lunches earlier on in the day while Jesus was still teaching? Did that account for twelve baskets being available?

We need to return to this theologian. What *was* the miracle in his eyes? Oh, yes! The little boy had shamed them out of their selfishness – an explanation included in a manual of approved teaching for trainee preachers.

But is the explanation plausible? It certainly does not explain the comment of Jesus the following day, does it? 'You are looking for Me because you ate the bread and had all you wanted, not because you understood My miracles'.[15] Unless, of course, one believes the 'miracle' of 'being shamed out of their selfishness' was what attracted them to seek more of the same medicine the next day? I'm sure your assessment of human nature, like mine, is that we are particularly averse to any such public exposure of our secret sins. Let's face facts. They followed Him because they 'ever more wanted that bread'!

Many in our 'enlightened scientific age' scoff at miracles; and they do so, all too often, without having a personal, intimate knowledge of God, or a personal experience of miracles. Not surprisingly then, many trend-setting clergy and pastors, as well as theologians and bishops, come to terms with 'worldly opinion' by watering down the Gospel. They do so in the supposed hope of making it more acceptable to the worldly-wise. I have had personal experience of this.

After the manuscript for *Rain in a Dry Land*[16] had been accepted in principle, an editor – not the one assigned to deal with my book – explained that my story would pose problems for many church people in this country because it spoke of too many 'miracles'! He said much of the antagonism had been brought about by 'a turning against' Wimber-type (signs-and-miracles-following) ministries. So as not to antagonise these people too much, I was asked to cut out quite a number of the miracles from my story. I was very unhappy about that decision. But I was assured that if I did that, the story itself – with fewer miracles – would be more likely to convince the doubters. Very unhappily (feeling that I had no alternative if I wanted to have the book published) I agreed to consider pruning the book of most miracles. When I explained this to the family and a number of people in our church fellowship at Theydon Bois, we agreed to pray that God would overrule this decision, believing each and every miracle to be an integral part of the story that

The Wilderness Experience

God wanted me to tell.

For six weeks I worked with a heavy heart on that pruning exercise. At the end of that time I had the most wonderful telephone call from Juliet, the person who helped me so enormously as my editor in getting the book into print. Apparently other editors had read the manuscript by this time, and the consensus of opinion was they now did not want me to remove any of those stories. Alleluia! Instead, they asked if I would mind adding another couple of chapters to further explain other events mentioned in the book.

But the incident speaks of a very real problem faced by 'Church' publishing houses, individual Christians and Christian leaders. In congregation after congregation I find many who believe in miracles face ostracism and ridicule even from their own pastors. The converse is also true; church leaders ridiculed by some in their congregations if they themselves believe in a miracle-working God.

The problem is *not* with an unbelieving world out there. It is far more serious than that. It is those within the Church itself (particularly the vocal and influential) who cannot find it in their hearts to believe in a God who intervenes in human history – miraculously!

Take heart. It was no different in the time of Jesus. John the Baptist was particularly uncompromising and brutal when dealing with the unfaithful, unbelieving church leaders of his day: 'You snakes! Who told you that you could escape from the punishment God is about to send?'[17] Harsh indeed! Jesus was equally so. He spoke of Jewish church leaders as 'whited sepulchres'(beautifully painted on the outside, but covering up stinking or lifeless remains within). He was furious with leaders who misled those entrusted to their care: 'If anyone should cause one of these little ones to lose his faith in Me, it would be better for that person to have a large millstone tied round his neck and be drowned in the deep sea. How terrible for the world that there are things that make people lose their faith! Such things will always happen – but how terrible for the one who causes them!'[19]

Much of our education system today is built on a false premise. The false premise is importance of pride in our own abilities and accomplishments and is false because it largely ignores our need for, and dependence on, God.

Much has been said in this chapter about doubt and unbelief. We can be crippled by them. There is a need to return to the desert. The timid church of Britain today,[20] as some have described it, speaks volumes for that organisation's lack-lustre, powerless, even impotent image in reaching our generation. It is a church that by and large continues (even prefers?) to live in the wilderness.

Archbishop Runcie, speaking of the Renewal of the 1960s and 1970s, said:

> If some of the spies sent out to reconnoitre 'the signs, wonders and miracles' of the Promised Land appear to correct Anglican eyes to have gone native with Rahab, perhaps that is because the main body of the Church of England seems to have forgotten the pioneers it sent out and [appears] to be marching back into the wilderness for another forty years.[21]

The Church will live in the wilderness until, in obedience to God's Word and commands, the Holy Spirit once again directs its life. God seeks a new generation that firmly believes *the impossible to be possible . . . with Him.*

Take heart! Even a desert (like the wilderness of Sinai) has much to commend it. It was Edward Pusey, well-known for his involvement in the founding of the Oxford Movement in the 19th century, who said:

> It is only afar off that the wilderness looks a waste,
>   and terrible and dry.
>
> Was it not there that a man did eat angel's food
>   and water gushed out of a rock
>   and bitter waters were made sweet . . . ?
>
> There shalt thou speak to God 'face-to-face'

and hear what the Lord thy God shall speak to thee.
There He shall renew thy soul
    hear thy prayer and answer it
    shed hope round thee
    kindle thy half-choked love
    give thee some taste out of His own boundless love

And give thee longing to pass out of all besides –
    out of thy decayed self gathered up to Him

Who came down to earth to our misery, to bear us up to
    Himself and make us one spirit with Him![22]

We all negotiate 'desert' experiences in our walk with God, and in working with other Christians. That has been very true for us in coming to work in a new country. We have had to deal with cultural changes, and much more besides. They have greatly tested our faith! Some of the following chapters will show we have learnt much about the very practical issues of coping with doubt and unbelief, and the need for God's supernatural intervention in so many areas of our lives.

NOTES:
[1] Numbers 14:9
[2] Psalm 68:1 (*RSV; New American Standard Bible*)
[3] Numbers 20:8
[4] Exodus 14:15 (*Living Bible*)
[5] Numbers 20:8
[6] Numbers 20:12
[7] ibid.
[8] Numbers 2 records there were over 600,000 able-bodied men – without taking account of wives, children, and those who would have been too old to fight.
[9] Deuteronomy 29:5
[10] Joshua 1:5
[11] Joshua 1:6–7, and 9
[12] Johua 3:3–5 and 13
[13] Joshua 3: 16b to the end
[14] *Daily Mail* (late 1984?)

To Reign or Not to Reign

[15] John 6:26
[16] *Rain in a Dry Land*, published by Hodder and Stoughton 1987
[17] Luke 3:7
[18] Matt. 23:27 (*KJV*)
[19] Matt. 18:6–8
[20] e.g. *The Church of England (Where is it going?)* by David Holloway, and published by Kingsway (1985); and *The Church in Crisis* by Charles Moore, A.N. Wilson and Gavin Stamp, published by Hodder and Stoughton (1986).
[21] Archbishop Robert Runcie – a comment made by him in connection with the Ecumenical Movement during a speech in General Synod in 1984. His actual statement was 'If some of the spies sent out to reconnoitre *the ecumenical* Promised Land appear to correct Anglican eyes to have gone native with Rahab, perhaps that is because, to them, the main body of the Church of England seems to have forgotten the pioneers it sent out and to be marching back into the wilderness for another forty years.' Rather than focusing on mistakes made, or on projects that had lost their way – and therefore encouraging denominations to withdraw from the scene altogether – Archbishop Runcie said, 'Let local ecumenical projects be judged by their best examples'. Surely, rather than retreating back into the wilderness, the same could be said of the 'rediscovery' of the Person, and of the Gifts, of the Holy Spirit – and all the good things that have stemmed from the Renewal Movement? And why not take that too a step further: 'Let the manifestations of the signs and wonders and miracles be judged by their best examples'.
[22] Source unknown

Chapter 3

DOUBT AND UNBELIEF

Even those of us who lived on another continent way below the equator in Zimbabwe had heard the statements of David Jenkins, Bishop of Durham. His non-acceptance of traditionally accepted teachings of the Creeds such as the Virgin Birth, the physical Resurrection of Christ, and His Second Coming were, and are, well known. Cartoons lampooning his position in the British Press were faithfully reproduced in our own national newspapers.

What surprised me on my arrival in this country was the higher than expected level of support the Bishop appeared to have amongst those in church leadership.

Not only do many of these not believe God would transgress natural law (so disposing of all signs and miracles), but also do not believe in Hell, or in the devil's existence (so no need for anyone to be concerned about the after-life). God by His very nature of goodness and love, they would argue, ensures everyone eventually goes to Heaven.

Some clearly have a problem accepting the uniqueness of Jesus. No wonder there is strong support for multi-faith worship, for they see all religions as equally valid paths to God. If that were so, then what was the point of Jesus' death, resurrection and ascension? Taking multi-faith worship and all that it implies a step further, they see no need to evangelize those of other faiths. So they effectively deny the uniqueness of Jesus, and His statement, 'no one goes to the Father, except by Me'.[1]

These people would have us exclude from the Bible all references to Hell, or the devil, or the division of sheep and goats, or statements referring to eternal separation from God! The question has to be asked how they reach such conclusions when many of the Biblical miracles, and much of the clear teaching about Hell, Satan, and eternal separation or damnation are ascribed to Jesus Himself?

The answer they would give is that it has to do with their understanding of what is acceptable belief! But to proclaim what is fundamentally opposed to Scripture – which is what this teaching is – is heresy.

No wonder the pronouncements of some Church of England leaders leave people furious or floundering. All those in Holy Orders have given an oath of allegiance to uphold the 'faith once delivered to the saints'. At the ordination to the Diaconate and the Priesthood, and in the consecration of a bishop, the candidates give an oath of allegiance. It is sworn on the Bible on each occasion, in one form of words or another. In the oath the person declares not only his acceptance of these teachings, but that he would also uphold and teach no other:

> I declare my belief in the faith which is revealed in the holy Scriptures and set forth in the Catholic Creeds and to which the historic formularies [*] of the Church of England bear witness . . .
> [* These are: The Prayer Book, the Thirty Nine Articles, and The Ordering of Bishops, Priests and Deacons]

All the formularies underscore the importance of *Scripture alone* as the foundation on which all teaching of the faith is formulated. This was determined at the time of the Reformation in all the major confessions: Augsburg, Westminster, and the Anglican 'all embracing historic formularies'. (See above).

The C. of E. speaks of three strands as essential for determining truth – Scripture, Reason and Tradition; and to teach nothing unless it can be concluded and proved by the Scriptures. Scripture is still the base line.

Liberal theologians would argue that *reason* is the most important of the three strands. Reason – what is or is not reasonable – is of course the basis of all *humanist* philosophies. What humanists and liberal theologians are saying is that we can only be expected to accept and believe what modern scientific man finds reasonable. To put it another way, God is reduced to the limits of what modern man sees as reasonable. Nothing less, in fact, than the making of God in our own image![2]

Liberal theology has certainly gained a strong foothold in the western Church. Is it therefore surprising that of the whole Christian Church worldwide, the Church in the west is not only the most lifeless, and powerless – but the only major part of the Church visibly dying in front of our eyes? This has certainly been true of Britain over the last century, and for most of our continental neighbours. In these countries many churches are practically empty on Sunday mornings!

For the liberal theologian, man's reason takes precedence over the authority of Scripture. I wonder if these words of Scripture ring any bells: 'God in His wisdom made it impossible for people to know Him by means of their own wisdom. Instead, by means of the so-called "foolish" message we preach, God decided to save those who believe'[3], – and, 'Those who are wise will turn out to be fools, and all their cleverness will be useless'.[4]

Reason for the liberal theologian is paramount. To them, that is what governs their interpretation, and acceptance, of Scripture. David Jenkins once defended his beliefs by saying: 'My position on the Virgin Birth [he doesn't believe Mary *was* 'virgo intacto'] and the bodily Resurrection [he does not believe it was] is based on Biblical interpretation and theological understanding *which have become well established over the last hundred years*'.

Does that necessarily make it any more true? The 'theological understanding' to which Jenkins refers takes account of a number of theories that have, over the last hundred years, carried much weight. These include considerable doubt on the dating of the first three gospels, their source and content.[5] Perhaps of even greater significance, is the almost universal acceptance – in liberal schools (emanating from certain German schools of thought) – that John's Gospel, and other writings of his, were NOT written by John at all, but most probably written in the second half of the second century. That is, about 150 years after the actual events! For that reason, they give less weight, less credence, to quotations in John's Gospel! The Bishop fails to mention more recent German scholars suggesting the original German schools worked from some false suppositions! This new school of thought believes John's Gospel *was* written by John himself, and at about the time of the other three Gospels![6]

Edward King, a former Dean of Cape Town (South Africa's version of Bishop Jenkins) when asked why he could not accept the literal truth of the Bible, replied:

> I think in terms of what modern scientific man can accept and believe, and what modern scholars today, in increasing numbers, have come to believe about presuppositions in Biblical times, and in the New Testament in particular. You know, I personally don't believe that Jesus walked across the lake, though I think the fact that it was recorded is very important!

'Very important'? Why would a false statement (that has to be the inference) be important!

Doubt creeps in because we are human. Doubt is the basis of the methodology the world uses in thinking of God, or about matters of faith, or interpretation of Scripture. It is *the world's way* of looking at things that has largely determined the pattern of much of the Church's thought processes.

Bishop Leslie Newbiggin, not, I hasten to add, a liberal theologian, argues that 'theological' education has failed Christian ministry because it is based on these self-same, false assumptions of a secular university: 'It is not that it is too academic. It is simply conducted on the basis of a set of unexamined assumptions which the Bible itself [God's word to mankind] calls into question'.[7]

What Christians, and theologians in particular, need to do, says Bishop Leslie Newbiggin, is to do an about turn and start looking out at the world from within the Bible! What Christians must do is take those Scriptural teachings and promises at face value, and then see where that leads. We will then begin to look at, and act, on things *from God's perspective* – and NOT from the perspective of our secular universities. However, we all too easily fall into a trap that Paul warned us about. But more of that in the next chapter.

NOTES:
[1] John 14:6
[2] e.g. Judges 17:6; 21:25
[3] 1 Cor. 1:21
[4] Isaiah 29:14
[5] See John Wenham in *Redating Matthew, Mark and Luke* (Hodder and Stoughton 1991)
[6] Martin Hengel, Professor of New Testament and Early Judaism, University of Tubingen, Germany: *The Johannine Question* (SCM 1989) and *The Hellenisation of Judaea in the 1st Century after Christ*
Re. The Johannine Question, for instance, Hengel says . . . 'unfortunately the later "critical censors" (the like of Bultmann) never went into the arguments of the doyens of German historical and critical New Testament scholarship . . . all the more reason why we should again listen to them more than we have done *in a time of widespread methodological confusion in the exegesis of John*' and that this should be all the more the case '*as the discovery of new texts now makes it impossible for us to give a late dating to the Johannine corpus*' (page 87)
[7] Bishop Leslie Newbiggin reported in *Church of England Newspaper (CEN)* 15 December 1989

Chapter 4

RESURRECTION POWER?

With a real gift of prophetic utterance, St Paul warned the Church:
'... in the last days ... [the people] will hold to the outward form of religion, but reject its power'.[1]

Many are doing just that today by their rejection of signs, wonders, miracles (and God's power to perform the same), and their rejection of those statements of the Creed that infer God's miraculous intervention – past, present or future.

No wonder Scripture goes on to say: 'The time will come when people will not listen to sound doctrine, but will follow their own desires and will collect for themselves more and more teachers who will tell them what they are itching to hear . . .'[2]

Today a diminishing number of people in the UK and Europe would look to the Church in their search for God, particularly a God who could give meaning to their lives; a God they could not only trust, but one who has power to intervene and improve their lives.

Why should this be so? Paul, in writing to Timothy said,

> Remind your people . . . give them a solemn warning in God's presence not to fight over words. It does no good, but only ruins the people who listen. Do your best . . . as a worker . . . who correctly teaches the truth . . . Don't copy Hymanaeus and Philetus who 'have left the way of truth and are upsetting the faith of some believers' by their heretical teaching, including false

teaching on the Resurrection.[3]

The writer to the Hebrews said something similar:

Let us go forward . . . to mature teaching and leave behind us the first lessons of the Christian message . . . we should not lay again the foundation of turning away from useless works and believing in God; of the teaching about baptism and the laying on of hands; of the resurrection of the dead and eternal judgement. Let us go forward![4]

And yet today, in the Church of the Western world there are leaders who not only question, but deny those basic tenets of the Christian faith. They deny the Virgin birth, Christ's physical resurrection from the dead, and the promise of His second coming. Is it any wonder then that there is confusion within the ranks, and a powerless church? Clearly it sends out some very disturbing signals to the man in the street!

Do these 'unbelieving' leaders of the Church have a point? One of the problems we will address concerns the Resurrection appearances of Jesus. The problem is that no one was initially able to recognise Jesus by His voice, His facial features, or in any of the normal ways we would expect to identify someone we love when they first met with Him after the resurrection. Why? There needs to be a plausible explanation if people are to take Scripture seriously. That is one issue, and we will deal with it in greater depth in the next chapter. But another issue is this: why is there so much doubt and unbelief within the Church?

The media have made much of the massive decline in church membership in all denominations of the Christian church over the last hundred years. But to get it in its right persepctive, that is only true of the largely affluent countries of the western world. It is not true in many parts of the third world where Christianity is growing at an astonishing rate. And at least one answer is not hard to find. In those areas the preaching of the Gospel is often followed by lives dramatically changed by God's power, and by startling signs. Here the signs of 'power-anointing' reflect the experiences of the early Christian church. Perhaps a reason for this is that, unlike our society, they have few 'hang-ups' about believing in a miracle-working God. What a contrast that is to the attitude and response of so many western church members!

So why this malaise in the West? Surprisingly, it is not that western society has become atheistic. Far from it. A look at the market place reveals something quite thought-provoking. A visitor to any general bookshop will usually have difficulty finding any Christian books on the shelves, apart perhaps from the odd Bible, prayer book or child's book of Bible stories stuck away in a remote corner. But what they WILL often find is a disproportionately large section relating to the occult and to other religions – and very often in a most prominent position in the shop.

If one remarks on this imbalance to the bookshop manager – or asks why books on witchcraft, the 'stars', the occult, the New Age movement and the eastern religions have such a high profile in the shop, they will be given a disturbing answer. Books on these subjects are more popular, and provide a much more significant part of their sales.

New Age groups (for New Age embraces all religions and none, all dimensions of the occult included) openly speak about power sources. THIS is what so many seek. It is not so much 'power' for its own sake, although that does play a part, but as proof that there is a cosmic power capable of shaping and controlling life. For this reason some believe reading of horoscopes will give guidance, and warnings, and knowledge of the future.

Just think about it. Almost every newspaper, magazine, radio and TV programme etc. gives a higher profile to this one area – 'Your Life in the Stars' – than to any Christian message. Again, if you ask why, the answer is crystal clear: the sheer volume of public demand. It's what people want!

The same is true of tarot cards, Ouija boards and all manner of occult activities, devil-worship included. However unpalatable these facts are to Christians, it is not that western men and women have turned away from God. What they *have* turned away from is a lacklustre Christian

To Reign or Not to Reign

faith. Why? Because the perception is that church is dry, boring, dull, lifeless and powerless to bring about anything worthwhile in people's lives!

Yes, the Church is seen, and portrayed, as a spent force; it is epitomised by the ridiculous caricatures of parsons that we so often see portrayed in the media. These endorse the meaningless drivel the general public expect the church to offer if they are stupid enough to venture in! Many who work in and through the media, and many out there 'in the real world' (as opposed to the 'fantasy' world they see the church to be) are atheists or agnostics who have no concept of what the church offers. They certainly have little or no time for it. But whose fault is that?

Listen to what one of them had to say: 'Organised religion has sunk pretty low these days, at least among people I know; the feeling is that it's just third-raters who get involved, oily little tin-pot careerists or neurotics, people afraid of the modern world . . .'[5] The writer of the article was attending a Baptism service! Part way through that same article he wrote: 'I can't believe this: I'm cringing, I want to escape. What have I got mixed up in here? These people, like druids round a campfire, warding off evil spirits . . . And they really said it: 'I renounce evil'! . . . Now we are standing up to sing a song [it happened to be a well-known traditional hymn.] . . . I'm squirming, can't get the words out. At the end I'm bolting for the door . . . Outside the church, the noisy irreligious world looks great. And no, I didn't get God.'[6]

He described pastors (?) as 'oily little tin-pot careerists'. In doing so, he painted a vivid picture of so many 'parson' caricatures. Many a truth is spoken in jest, we are told. Would New Testament pastors have been so described? Certainly not, the opposite was true. So many dramatic things happened as they preached and ministered – causing such a challenge to society and the established 'Church' – that there was nothing 'tin-pot' about them. They were anything but 'oily'. Their message was clear and uncompromising. We could learn a lesson or two there.

S.J. Forrest (speaking as he was of his own C. of E. – but true of

Resurrection Power?

most main-stream churches) puts it succinctly:

> By doctrines obliquely averred,
> And slightly ambiguous phrase,
> We marshall our dissonant herd,
> The blacks and the whites and the greys.
>
> Whenever required to affirm
> A dogma of Heaven or Hell,
> We use an equivocal term,
> To cover denials as well.
>
> When questioners ask for advice,
> We find it prudent to swerve,
> By answering, 'It shall suffice
> As every man's conscience may serve . . .'
>
> It diddles the devil, we know,
> And baffles his sinister ends;
> He cannot tell if he's a foe
> Or one of our intimate friends . . .[7]

That about sums up how 'the world out there' sees the Church's belief structure; so there can be no surprise that they find it lifeless, dead, boring, and powerless. What is more, its archaic traditions, 'unworldly' dress and, for many, its music are seen as long past their sell-by date, living in a time warp! That is the nub of it. What an indictment against an organisation charged with representing the living, all-powerful God of this universe, an organisation that thereby, on a massive scale, fails in its primary purpose of reaching and winning those very people to the living Christ! Is it surprising, in these circumstances, that those very people have neither interest in, nor time – let alone respect – for the Church?

Yet paradoxically, we have the most priceless treasure ever revealed.

We, as Christians, see Jesus in the God who loves and cares for this broken world, and who gave His Son to be a ransom for many. This Jesus lived and died gloriously, and through the power of His Resurrection is now alive and intercedes for us. More! He enters the lives of those willing to respond to Him, offering them a new and personal relationship with Himself. He gives them a peace, dignity and strength for a new beginning. Here, instead of the human philosophies of the world's religions, we are offered a vibrant faith and intimate relationship with the living God. A God who meets people at their point of need, and who has the power to transform their lives and situations for good.

So where are the unmistakable signs of that power at work in the Church today? Peter and John, empowered as they were, revealed those unmistakable signs when Peter spoke to the cripple at the entrance to God's house. I can't give you silver or gold! But: '"I give you what I have: in the name of Jesus Christ of Nazareth I order you to get up and walk." Then he took him by his right hand and helped him up. At once the man's feet and ankles became strong; he jumped up, stood on his feet, and started walking around. Then he went into the temple with them, walking and jumping and praising God'.[8]

Here was a walking testimony to the power God. Furthermore, the demonstration of such a power-filled ministry so threatened the Temple authorities that they had to take immediate steps to try to nip the challenge to their own lacklustre ministries in the bud. Would it be any different today? Can you imagine churchwardens, deacons or elders allowing someone to exuberantly praise God aloud, and leap around within the church? Not on your life – certainly not in most churches!

The Temple leaders asked by 'what power' or in 'whose name' the apostles had performed this amazing act of miraculous healing. The answer was quite clear – through the power Jesus had given them. Clearly the challenge – (showing up 'the old order' for the impotent power it had become?) – had to be contained immediately. So they prohibited Peter and John from ever again speaking in the name of Jesus.[9] Is it any different today?

Resurrection Power?

But Peter and John were not only empowered. They knew Jesus, and knew what He expected of them. Jesus certainly did not want them to run like frightened rabbits the moment they faced fierce opposition. They were soon found with the other disciples praying: '"... Lord take notice of the threats they have made, and allow us Your servants, to speak Your message with all boldness. Stretch out Your hand to heal, and grant that wonders and miracles may be performed through the name of your holy Servant Jesus". The place where they were meeting was shaken. They were all filled [for the second time![10]] with the Holy Spirit . . .'[11]. That is what we should be doing in our churches today, and doing it even when church leaders, or other members of the church, try to stifle the work of the Spirit.

When I speak of the need for a believing, power-filled Church today, I am often challenged by bishops, clergy and ministers. The reason? One could cause such disappointment if nothing resulted from the prayers (for healing, for instance). The solution they would offer? It would be better to remain silent and not raise false hope. No wonder Jesus cried: 'O faithless generation'[12] . . . how long do I have to put up with your unbelief?

Most of us have a problem with doubt and unbelief. But Jesus can meet us at that point if we ask Him. Thomas experienced just that sort of doubt after the Resurrection; he simply found it impossible to believe! So when Jesus met up with him, He said: 'Put your finger here, and look at My hands; then stretch out your hand and put it in My side. Stop your doubting, and believe!'[13]

What followed from Thomas was the ultimate recognition of who Jesus really was: 'My Lord and my God!'[14]

And Jesus said to Thomas: 'Do you believe because you see Me? How happy are those who believe without seeing Me.'[15]

James, too, has a wonderful passage on the need for faith, and the exercise of it:

You do not have what you want because you do not ask God for it. And when you ask, you do not receive it, because your motives are bad . . . So then, submit to God. Resist the devil, and he will run away from you. Come near to God, and He will come near to you . . . Are any of you in trouble? You should pray. Are any of you happy? You should sing praises. Are any of you ill? You should send for the church elders, who will pray for them and rub olive-oil on them in the name of the Lord. This prayer made in faith will heal the sick; the Lord will restore them to health, and the sins they have committed will be forgiven.[16]

I believe our prayers are always answered, but not always in the way we would hope or expect. For God is sovereign, and in each individual situation He knows the person's deepest needs – and so His agenda, for healing for instance, may often be the need to deal initially with emotional or spiritual factors before physical healing takes place. What God DOES require of us is that we pray in faith, and that we take God's promises at face value!

The specifics of knowing what to pray for – and how to pray in God's will, will be dealt with at greater length in a later chapter. We will make mistakes – but that must not prevent our stepping out in faith: 'be not faithless',[17] but a believing people. THAT is what honours God!

One further point needs to be noted. Many find it virtually impossible to believe that the God of the whole universe would work a miracle for 'me'! What, here and now, and for my particular situation or need? And when asked to pray for someone's total healing, the response would go something like this: 'It would take a saint to work a miracle like that, and I'm no saint'

These two issues are closely connected – doubt and unbelief on the one hand and, on the other, God powerfully at work in and through even 'me'!

Paul says to his readers:'For even though it was in weakness that He was put to death on the cross, it is by *God's power* that He lives. In union with Him we also are weak; but in our relations with you we shall share *God's power* in His life.'[18]

Resurrection Power?

Paul has a very powerful message for us, for today's Church. It runs like a gold thread through his letters, and in the events recorded for us in the Acts of the Apostles. That thread underlines and emphasises, in wonderful and practical ways, all that Jesus Himself taught and promised us: 'Believe Me when I say that I am in the Father and the Father is in Me. If not, believe because of the things I do. I am telling you the truth: those who believe in Me *will* do what I do – yes, they will do even greater things because I am going to the Father. And I will do whatever you ask for in My name, so that the Father's glory will be shown through the Son. If you ask for anything in My name, I will do it'.[19]

What sensational promises! Can we believe them?

Paul wants us to know they *are* believable. Paul's special prayer was: 'that you will know . . . how very great is His power at work in us who believe. This power working in us' [wait for it!] 'is the same as the mighty strength which He used when He raised Christ from death'.[20]

Paul identifies both the source and the greatness of that power. Again, can we believe it? Paul 'underlines' the promise again further on in the same letter:

> . . . who by means of His power working in us is able to do so much more than we can ever ask for, or even think of . . .'[21] and yet again, the power God makes available to His Church is the same power that raised Jesus from the dead: ' . . . finally build up your strength in union with the Lord and by means of His mighty power . . .'[22] The same claim is also made in Paul's letter to the Colossians: 'May you be made strong with all the strength which comes from His glorious power . . .'[23]

He continually stresses that this 'power that raised Jesus' is for the members of Christ's Church. For us! But for some, the crucial issue still to be tackled, is: 'What if Jesus did not rise physically from the dead?'

A book that has helped many in this area of doubt is Frank Morison's classic, *Who Moved the Stone*. It certainly helped me when I was at

University in the 1950s. More recently I came across some interesting information about Frank Morison. Despite what I was told then, Frank Morison was not a lawyer! What is more, the name under which he wrote was not his own, but a pseudonym. His real name was Albert Henry Ross, and he worked for an advertising agency. But lawyer or not, he showed how legal investigative skills could be effectively used to 'sift the evidence' available to us.

His original purpose in writing the book was to prove Jesus did NOT rise from the dead. But as all his readers know, he was finally forced to the conclusion – from checking out all the evidence available to him – that Jesus did rise from the dead on the third day![24] So Frank Morison was not a lawyer. But many lawyers and eminent judges *have* reviewed all the evidence and come to similar conclusions.

In 1970, Sir Leslie Heron, Chief Justice of New South Wales in Australia, said:

> Let any objective reader put side by side the four gospels and add to them the account in the Acts of the Apostles and he will be struck, as any judge accustomed to evaluate evidence is always struck, with one outstanding fact. It is this: that while there may be a great variety of detail or form of expression or narration or of emphasis put on occurrences, underneath it all the substance and weight of the narration are true.[25]

Many have said the eleven disciples could not possibly have all lied about the Resurrection, and gone on living that lie – even to the extent of being prepared to die for a lie, without someone 'spilling the beans'. A lawyer who hit the headlines – but from the other side of the fence so to speak – bears that out. He was Charles Colson, implicated and imprisoned for his involvement in the Watergate affair. He says: "Take it from one who was inside the Watergate web looking out, who saw firsthand how vulnerable a cover-up is. Nothing less than a witness as awesome as the resurrected Christ could have caused those men to maintain to their dying whispers that Jesus is alive and Lord.'[26]

Resurrection Power?

John Stott, well known evangelical leader in this country, tells of the findings of Sir Edward Clarke:

> As a lawyer I have made a prolonged study of the evidences of the events of the first Easter Day. To me the evidence is conclusive, and over and over again in the High Court I have secured the verdict on evidence not nearly so compelling. Inference follows on evidence, and a truthful witness is always artless and disdains effect. The Gospel evidence for the Resurrection is of this class and, as a lawyer, I accept it unreservedly as the testimony of truthful men to facts they were able to substantiate.[27]

Many such testimonies are to be found in an excellent booklet *Leading Lawyers Look at the Resurrection* by Ross Clifford.[28] It is a book that can be given in confidence to those who question the Resurrection, or indeed the authenticity of Scripture.

But, as we all know only too well, you can sometimes talk to someone until you are 'blue in the face' without convincing them – whatever the 'facts'! The problem for many of us is the ability to move a stage further – even when we have taken account of 'the facts' – and have made it a matter of personal belief.

It was Dale Foreman (this will be the last legal quote!) who said:

> These facts (detailing the trial, crucifixion and death of Jesus), I believe, are clear and proven beyond reasonable doubt. Whether you can take one step further and believe the miracle of the Resurrection is something only you can decide. Still, the reliability of the rest of the Gospels is so plain that it is but a small step to believe in the resurrected Christ. And what's more, it would be hard to believe that a man could have such an influence on the world if he had not overcome the ultimate enemy – death.[29]

So, with so much weighty evidence to hand, why do so many within the church – and very specially those in leadership positions – still have doubts about Jesus' physical resurrection?

Despite being convinced of it by Frank Morison's book,[30] for years I still had questions I couldn't answer. I knew that Jesus must have risen physically from the dead. But the disquiet remained because, as a preacher and teacher of the Christian faith, I discovered I was actually fearful of people asking questions about something that seemed totally inconsistent with real-life experience. And the problem was this.

In reading all the Resurrection stories, the one disquieting factor in each story is the fact that no single person – although so closely connected to Jesus before His death – was initially able to recognise Him by

His voice,
His hair,
His facial features, or in
any way we normally identify someone we love.

Why? How can that be explained?

For years this caused me concern. And then years later, as a result of an extraordinary chain of events, I was given what I can only describe as an understanding, or 'revelation'. What was shown to me not only resolved the whole issue for me, but revealed things about Jesus' victory on the cross I had not understood before. It was a 'mind-blowing' experience . . .

More about that next.

NOTES:
[1] 2 Tim.3: 1b,5
[2] 2 Tim.4:3
[3] 2 Tim.2:14ff
[4] Hebrews 6:1–3
[5] William Leith in the *Independent*, Sunday 30th August, 1992
[6] ibid.
[7] S.J. Forrest in *What's the Use* (Mowbrays 1955) Page 18
[8] Acts 3: 6b–8
[9] Acts 4:7–18

Resurrection Power?

[10] See Acts 2:4 for first 'filling'.
[11] Acts 4:29–31
[12] Matt. 17:17 (*KJV*); also Mark 9:19, Luke 9:41
[13] John 20:27
[14] John 20:28b
[15] John 20:29
[16] James 4:2b, 3, 7 & 8a; 5:13–15
[17] John 20:27 (*KJV*)
[18] 2 Cor. 13:4
[19] John 14:11–14
[20] Eph.1: 18b, 19, 20a
[2] Eph.3:20
[22] Eph.6:10
[23] Col.1:11
[24] Frank Morison in *Who moved the Stone?* (IVP, 1982) Pages 89 and 193
[25] Sir Leslie Heron in *The Trial of Jesus of Narareth from a Lawyer's Point of View* (The Australian Lawyer's Christian Fellowship 1970) Page 1.
[26] Charles Colson in *Loving God* (Marshalls 1984) Page 69.
[27] Cited by John Stott in *Basic Christianity* (IVP 1974), Page 47.
[28] Ross Clifford, *Leading Lawyers Look at the Resurrection* published by Albatross Books Pty. Ltd. (Lion Publishing in the UK) 1991.
[29] Dale Foreman in *Crucify Him: A Lawyer looks at the Trial of jesus* (Zondervan 1990), Page 176.
[30] *Who Moved the Stone?* (IVP)

Chapter 5

RESURRECTION: FACT OR FANTASY?

What did Jesus look like? In Isaiah we are told 'He had no dignity or beauty to make us take notice of Him.'[1] This is a very different picture from that given in twentieth century film epics where He is usually portrayed as a particularly handsome Caucasian – with long and attractive auburn hair! The Isaiah passage, describing Him as having 'no dignity or beauty to make us take notice of Him',[2] has been explained by some commentators as follows: since He was not a handsome person, people would not commit the sin of envy when they looked at Him! Maybe so, maybe not. What is not in doubt is that He *did* attract large crowds to Himself – such was His personality, His teaching, His bearing, and because He performed such startling miracles. In those ways He was certainly 'attractive'. He had the kind of credit rating given to present day megastars.

Whatever Jesus may have looked like (and we can note that we recognise people by their looks, physical features, voice and so on) none of His close friends recognised Him by any of these features after His death. That is startling. Is there an explanation?

In Matthew's Gospel we are told, 'The eleven disciples went to the hill in Galilee where Jesus had told them to go. When they saw Him, they worshipped Him, *even though some of them doubted*'.[3] That was forty days after the Resurrection! Several had seen Him on a number of occasions, so how could they still doubt? Either it was Him – the person whose life they had intimately shared day in and day out for at least three years – or it wasn't.

In Luke's Gospel[4] the facts are even more extraordinary. We are told a fascinating story in which two of Jesus' disciples (Cleopas and another – possibly his wife Mary?) walked seven or eight miles back home to Emmaus, a distance that would in all probability take them a couple of hours and more to cover. For most of that time they listened, and didn't recognise His voice, to a man they clearly 'saw' as a total stranger. In that talk 'Jesus explained to them what was said about Himself in all the Scriptures, beginning with the books of Moses and the writings of all the prophets'.[5] That must have taken some considerable time! Yet they were unable to identify Him by His voice, His physical features, the way He looked or smiled, or anything else. But that was not all. As it was practically nightfall when they arrived at Emmaus, they invited Him to come in and stay the night with them. Further discussion would no doubt have taken place in the house while a meal was being prepared.

It was only at supper, in the simple act of Jesus breaking the bread, that they suddenly realised who He was. And then He 'disappeared from their sight'. Then 'they said to each other, "Wasn't it like a fire burning in us when He talked to us on the road and explained the Scriptures to us?"'[6]

Those two rushed back to Jerusalem – all eight miles! – to let the disciples know they too had seen the Risen Lord. And no sooner had they recounted their amazing story, when Jesus appeared to all those gathered in that Upper Room. We are told they 'were terrified, thinking that they were seeing a ghost'.[7] Jesus' response is illuminating. 'Why are you alarmed? Why are these doubts coming up in your minds?'[8]

The only reason for doubt, as I understand it, is that they did not actually recognise the person they loved with any certainty. They hadn't recognised His voice when He said 'Peace be with you',[9] nor did His physical features, or His appearance give them the categorical assurance that it was Jesus.

This is borne out by what happens next. Instead of saying 'Look at Me' He says 'Look at My hands and My feet and see that it is I Myself'.[10] The print of the nails on hands and feet testified to this being the

Resurrection: Fact or Fantasy?

crucified Jesus!

'They still could not believe'![11] Why? Well, for a start they obviously had not expected to see Him again – He had died! They still hadn't come to terms with the possibility of a resurrection. And there was a further problem. Was the apparition simply a ghost? Remember doors and windows were locked and barred – yet this figure had arrived in the room. Jesus recognised this train of thought and so said to them: '"Have you anything here to eat?" They gave Him a piece of cooked fish which He took and ate in their presence'.[12] No ghost can do that! But the conclusions are clear – they only recognised their friend by the marks of the nails. And eating the fish proved He was no ghost.

In John's Gospel there are some further accounts. After the fantastic experience of actually meeting and speaking with angels, Mary Magdalene, we are told, '"turned round and saw Jesus standing there; but [although she had known Him so well in life] she did not know that it was Jesus. "Woman, why are you crying?" Jesus asked'.[13] What a question to ask of a grieving person at a tomb! Some suggest she didn't recognise Him because the flood of tears of this distraught woman would have blinded her. I don't believe that. However much a person has been weeping, the face of a loved one is instantly recognised as one to whom one can turn. And what follows next seems to rule this out. 'Who is it that you are looking for?'[14] This is the second time He has spoken to her, yet she has no inkling that it is *His* voice! '"She thought He was the gardener, so she said to Him, 'If you took Him away, sir, tell me where you have put Him, and I will go and get Him'"[15]

The 'Sir' could imply a man of some standing, or one considerably older than oneself. In Third World countries – as in Britain in days gone past – people much older than oneself are accorded a mark of respect when addressed as 'Father', 'Baba' or 'Sir'". But Jesus was only a young man in his early thirties!

However everything changed dramatically when Jesus spoke a third time – and all He said was the one word: 'Mary'![16] Only then did she instantly realise who He was. Why? It is possible that it was not so much the voice but perhaps the intonation or special endearment used

To Reign or Not to Reign

in the way He said 'Mary' that reminded her of Jesus. For was there not a somewhat higher than normal level of awe and intense excitement as she responded, '"Rabboni!"'? Suddenly it was beginning to sink in. He has risen! He's here with me now!

But up to this moment she had not recognised His face, His voice, or anything else about Him. Only that one word – her name – unlocked the gate of recognition!

John also tells the story of 'doubting' Thomas. Thomas had not been present that first Easter Sunday evening when Jesus had presented Himself to the band of disciples – Cleopas and his companion from Emmaus included. When they related the incident to him later in the week, Thomas refused to believe it. He said to them 'Unless I see the scars of the nails in His hands and put my finger on those scars and my hand in His side, I will not believe.'[17]

Jesus, gracious and understanding as always, met them a week later in the same room; this time Thomas was there too. 'The doors were locked, but Jesus came and stood among them.'[18] This habit of passing through walls in rooms where doors and windows were barred must have been quite frightening to those on the receiving end. They didn't have twentieth century science fiction – with films like *Star Trek*, and the possibility of 'beaming' crew members to other places – to help them come to terms with what they would have seen as a purely ghostly experience. So it wasn't surprising for the disciples to believe they were seeing an apparition. Jesus therefore 'showed them His hands and His side' and invited Thomas to actually touch the scars; not something you can do with a ghost!

But can you imagine what that suggestion did to Thomas? Jesus telling him to look at, and touch, the scars would have reminded him of that earlier meeting and his challenge to them: 'Unless I see the scars of the nails in His hands . . .'! And here was Jesus was telling him to do just that.

We will begin to understand better what was going on in Thomas' mind if we are able to understand the significance of what happened to Nathaniel. Do you remember the incident? Philip had persuaded

Resurrection: Fact or Fantasy?

Nathaniel to come and meet Jesus. Nathaniel was pretty scathing – 'Can anything good come from Nazareth?' 'Come and see', Philip encourages him. Shortly afterwards Nathaniel meets with Jesus. Jesus promptly says (of a man He had presumably never met before): 'Here is a real Israelite; there is nothing false in him'. Nathaniel is apparently amazed at the perceptiveness of Jesus' comment, and replies: 'How do you know me?' to which Jesus responds: 'I saw you when you were under the fig tree before Philip called you'.

Let's look at that story a moment. The significant point was *not* that Jesus saw Nathaniel standing under a fig tree. We often say to someone 'I saw you . . .' *That* fact is not significant. But it can take on real significance if it sparks an inner response in the person being addressed – like: 'Oh dear, he must have seen me going into . . . walking with . . . speaking to . . .' or whatever. It was clear that Jesus not only *saw* Nathaniel (whether in person, or in a vision matters not), but *knew* what he was *thinking* or *saying*. *That* is what startled Nathaniel. It came about through Jesus' spiritual gift of 'knowledge'. Such revelatory knowledge was so mind-blowing that all Nathaniel could say was: 'You are the Son of God! You are the King of Israel!'[20]

In the same way, Thomas suddenly understood. Like Nathaniel, all he could reply when Jesus showed him the marks of the nails, and the wound in His side, was 'My Lord and *my God.*'

The remark would not have been made simply because he saw the marks of crucifixion on that body. It was more than that. Why did he address his friend as 'God'? Was it because he now knew Jesus had indeed risen from the dead? Possibly. But could it have been more that? We will come back to that later.

There is one further incident to be noted – also recorded for us by John. Peter, with six others, had gone fishing overnight on Lake Galilee – and caught exactly nothing! 'As the sun was rising, Jesus stood at the water's edge, but the disciples did not know that it was Jesus.'[22] One reason for that non-recognition given by some commentators is that if one has a person standing with the rising sun immediately behind him, you cannot make out the person's features. All one sees is the outline of the person's head. But does that make sense of the quite extraordinary statement that follows?

Jesus asked them, 'Young men, haven't you caught anything?' For what possible reason would He address them as '*young*'? He Himself was little more than thirty years of age; older than John, certainly, but probably much the same age as others in the boat; possibly younger than some. So why on earth should He address them as 'young men', or 'children'?

The only logical answer that makes any sense is that Jesus automatically assumes, from *their* observation of *Him*, that He looks much older than He actually is! That, too, we'll look at later.

'"Young men, haven't you caught anything?" "Not a thing", they answered. He said to them, "Throw your net on the other side of the boat and you will catch some." So they threw the net out and could not pull it back in, because they had caught so many fish'.[24] Only then, we are told, did John the beloved disciple realize who it must be; he recognised Him because of the miracle of the fish. Peter, and no doubt John too, would have been reminded of a previous and very similar miracle near the start of Jesus' ministry.[25]

Have you noticed how the Bible never covers up peoples' shortcomings or failings? Not even those looked up to as the great prophets, kings or saints! We have a wonderful example of this right here. As soon as it dawned on Peter what John was saying – that this 'stranger' was Jesus – he did something that not only overturned a habit of a lifetime, but also revealed Peter's confused state at Jesus' appearance. When fishermen set out on their fishing trips, they took off most of their clothes and put them in a place where they would be kept dry. Recognising his near nakedness, Peter reached for his clothes. But instead of jumping into the water and holding them above his head until he reached the shore, he put them on . . . and then jumped into the water! He would not have lived that down for a long time!

The story doesn't end there. It continues: 'None of the disciples dared ask Him, "Who are you?", because they knew it was the Lord'.[25] The very way this is phrased implies the possibility of doubt. Why?

Resurrection: Fact or Fantasy?

The way we recognise people is by their physical features, voices, mannerisms and so on. Yet the clear and indisputable evidence of every one of these Gospel resurrection narratives points to the fact that these were the very signs they could *not* rely on!

Some commentators suggest He simply decided not to reveal Himself for some reason. Does that really make any sense? Or was it because His face, His hair and His voice were so changed as to be unrecognisable?

If that is so, what prevents anyone assuming the Resurrection was a hoax?

It was this particular problem that exercised my mind for many years. The 'plus' factor was the other side of the coin. If a group of people were really planning to hoodwink the world and try to pull off such a conspiracy – presuming Jesus failed them by not rising from the dead – they would have ensured they didn't put out apparently conflicting resurrection stories. Nor would they have recorded stories that left so many riddles unanswered – like, was it Jesus, or wasn't it?

Thinking back over these stories, we could summarise them like this:

i) At the time of Christ's ascension into Heaven, forty days after the resurrection, some still doubted.

ii) At Emmaus, after a two-hour walk and discussion, Jesus was only recognised in the breaking of bread.

iii) On Easter Sunday night in the barred Upper Room, Jesus was only recognised by the scars of the nails in hands and feet, and the realization He was not a ghost because He ate fish.

iv) Mary Magdalene only recognised Him by the word 'Mary'.

v) Thomas believed it was Jesus by seeing the scars of the nails. Further, he responded to what he saw by calling Jesus 'my God'.

vi) At the lakeside they didn't recognise Him except by the miracle of the fish. And Jesus addressed His friends as 'young' men!

So! In not one of these incidents did anyone recognise Him in any of the more conventional ways. Rather, the reverse was true. In these incidents they didn't recognise His features at all, and that included a distinctive and much-loved face, voice, and head of hair.

Instead, He revealed Himself:

in the 'breaking of bread',
in the way He said 'Mary',
in the miracle of fish, and by
showing the scars of the nails.

In eating a piece of fish, He dispelled any idea that He was simply a ghostly apparition – or of having only risen 'spiritually', and not physically.

A clue to finding a solution to this riddle – for me – first came during the guerilla war in Zimbabwe. It concerned people who endured horrendous shock and trauma as a result of some particularly gruesome or barbarous incident perpetrated against someone near and dear. The shock, in some cases, literally turned their hair white practically overnight. That, together with the fact that Jesus' hair is referred to more than once in Scripture as 'white', started a whole new train of thought.

I mentioned at the beginning of this chapter that Isaiah spoke of Jesus having 'no dignity or beauty to make us take notice of Him'.[27] In the previous chapter Isaiah describes Jesus in a way that is, prophetically, even more enlightening: 'Many people were shocked when they saw Him; He was so disfigured that He hardly [scarcely] looked human'.[28]

Over and over again, Scripture tells us that Christ, totally sinless, took all our sins upon Himself: 'to be sin for us, who knew no sin . . .';[29] and who 'carried our sins in His body to the cross, so that we might die to sin and live for righteousness. It is by His wounds that you have been healed'.[30]

Anyone committing a really grievous sin for the first time knows the sense of shame that it brings; it is inevitably followed by 'if only I could turn the clock back!' Imagine the effect of that multiplied millions of times to someone like Jesus who knew no sin! Further, each one of us has seen the ravages of what debauchery can do to a person. Amongst other things, they grow old before their time! It's not unusual for a habitual alcoholic or drug addict to be taken for a person ten, twenty or even thirty years older than they actually are.

So how would one quantify the possible ageing process for someone who was completely sinless willingly accepting the penalty of all the world's sin? Take note that it would also include the horrendous crimes of every tyrant, and of every serial killer and psychopath that ever lived.

Beacuse God cannot look on sin, the result of that action separated Jesus for the first time ever from the one He loved most of all – His Father. The result of that was the most heart-rending cry ever heard:

'My God, my God, why did You abandon Me? [why hast Thou forsaken me?]'[31]

One thing more needs to be considered. At His crucifixion, we are told that Jesus 'took our infirmities and bore our diseases'[32] or, as the Authorised Version puts it, 'took our infirmities, and bare our sicknesses'.

As I tried to understand this, all I could think of were the ravages that something like cancer or leprosy can do to disfigure a person beyond recognition. I saw the horrors of this in the Mtemwa Leper Colony I visited regularly in one of my parishes in Zimbabwe. I also remembered the enormous personal difficulties I faced – trying to disguise my own shock and the nausea rising within me, doing my best not to turn and run – when having to minister to a man in hospital whose mouth and nose had been eaten away by disease. His disfigurement did something else. The words he spoke were almost impossible to decipher. They didn't sound human, because he had lost the mouth 'chamber' that helps produce that distinctive sound when we speak.

Could it have been factors like this that so transformed Jesus' features, His face, His voice, and His hair as to make Him virtually unrecognisable?

And would this explain why, on some of those occasions, they only recognised Him when He showed them the marks of crucifixion? Would this explain

why His voice was unrecognisable, and
why only the one word 'Mary' was recognisable, or
why they recognised Him in the breaking of bread, or
why they recognised Him by the miracle of the fish ?

If, for a moment, we presume He now looked like a very old man, would this explain the riddle, and further explain why He addressed people His own age as 'young men' or 'children'?

In this last instance, the particular word in the original text (Greek: *Paidion*) is used when someone addresses little children; or when an older person, who commands respect because of age, speaks to younger people. It is the *only time*, despite the countless times He addresses His disciples in the Gospels that Jesus uses this particular Greek word *Paidion* to address them!

But what is clearly more important, can Scripture support these ideas or theories? John, probably the youngest of the apostles and the one 'Jesus loved' and who sat next to Him at the Last Supper, tried to find an explanation for those things. For something like the next fifty or sixty years he must have puzzled over those resurrection appearances, and all that they had observed of Jesus after His resurrection.

John, I believe, found the answer. When he was a very old man, and a prisoner on the island of Patmos, he tells us of a revelation he received from God:

On the Lord's Day the Spirit took control of me, and I heard a loud voice, that sounded like a trumpet, speaking behind me. It said, 'Write down what you see, and send the book to the churches'. [He goes on] I turned round to see who was talking to me, and I saw seven gold lampstands, and among them what *looked like* a human being, wearing a robe that reached to His feet, and a gold belt round His chest. His *hair* was *white* as wool, or as snow, and His eyes blazed like fire; His feet shone like brass that has been refined and polished, and His *voice* sounded like a roaring waterfall . . .[33]

Extraordinary, isn't it, when we look at it like that? Hair as white as snow! Eyes blazing like fire! He was 'what *looked like* a human being'! Would that be the same as 'scarcely looked human'? The voice was 'like a trumpet', or 'like a roaring waterfall'.

But when John tries to describe the *face* that had changed so dramatically after death as to make Jesus unrecognisable, he is lost for words. The only way he could try to explain this riddle was by saying: 'a sharp two-edged sword came out of His mouth . . .'

What a gruesome thought! Is that what it was meant to convey? I believe it was God's way of revealing the mystery. For several years I reflected on that and longed to know the meaning behind it. Then one day while I was praying about it, I was led to look at another passage in Scripture that appears to clearly explain the significance of a 'sharp two-edged sword' coming 'out of His mouth':

> The word of God is alive and active, sharper than any *double-edged sword.* It cuts all the way through, to where soul and spirit meet, to where joints and marrow come together. *It judges the desires and thoughts* of man's heart. There is nothing that can be hidden from God; *everything* in all creation is *exposed and lies open before His eyes.* And it is *to Him that we must all give an account of ourselves.*[34]

A complete revelation, perhaps, of all Jesus suffered physically, mentally and spiritually when he took the sins of all upon Himself on the Cross.

It's significant, isn't it, that in the picture we are given of Jesus coming back to judge the world in the last days, He is riding a white horse and 'out of His mouth came a sharp sword'![35]

That sight, of the sword in the first chapter of Revelation, was so mind-blowing, John tells us, that 'I fell down at His feet like a dead man. He [Jesus] placed His right hand on me and said, "Don't be afraid! I am the first and the last. I am the living one! I was dead, but now I am alive for ever and ever. I have authority over death and the world of the dead. Write, then, the things that you see . . ."'[36]

When we allow all that to sink in, it is incomprehensible that we treat sin so lightly. And to realise that He died, not of crucifixion, but because His heart was actually ruptured! He literally died of a broken heart. That has never been true of anyone else, although 'I'm heartbroken' or 'Someone's broken my heart' is a common enough saying! This is what our sin did to Jesus.

It was John again to whom we are indebted for this particular piece of information. Did he know exactly what it was he was recording? Or was it simply an unusual fact that did not fit in with their plentiful experience of what happened when people normally died as a result of crucifixion? This is what John records for us: 'Then the Jewish authorities asked Pilate to allow them to break the legs of the men who had been crucified, and to take the bodies down from the crosses . . .'[37]

Crucifixion was particularly gruesome because it usually took more than a day for a person to die. The only way to expedite the process is to break the legs. Doing so prevents the person so crucified lifting himself up to draw breath. This means the lungs fill more rapidly with moisture, thus speeding up the way people died when crucified – through pneumonia and suffocation. It is then that John records this extraordinary fact:

> But when they came to Jesus, they saw that He was already dead, so they did not break His legs. One of the soldiers, however, [presumably thinking Jesus might be faking death, because people rarely died that fast when crucified] plunged his spear into Jesus' side, and at once blood and water poured out. The one who saw this happen [that is, noting that blood, then water in that order, coming from His side] has spoken of it so that you also may

believe. What he said is true, and he knows that he speaks the truth'.[38]

If a person died of crucifixion (i.e. pneumonia and suffocation) and then a spear pierced the lungs and heart, what would be observed would be a flood of water followed by blood. You would not see blood followed by water – as John records it. In Jesus' case there was no flood of water. That is what amazed John. He noted the fact, but probably didn't know the significance of it. Only medical science in the twentieth century has been able to explain the significance of blood – then water – coming from the wound. The lung cavity had already filled with blood from a ruptured heart, before pneumonia (which fills the lungs with 'water') had set it.

What a Saviour! As God gave me an understanding of those passages, and an explanation that satisfied my earlier doubts about those Resurrection appearances, you may well imagine the amazement and joy I experienced. Scripture tells us the Holy Spirit will be our teacher and guide, and reveal mysteries to us. I believe He had done just that. God speaks through His word even to ordinary people like you and me.

On one occasion when I was sharing this at a Bible study with our Diocesan Missionary Council, someone asked: 'Do you think Jesus still bears those marks?'

I don't know. John, in the book of Revelation, shows Jesus as bearing them. In a magnificent hymn written by David Fellingham,[39] he says all that needs to be said as he picks up the words of John's vision:

At Your feet we fall, mighty risen Lord,
As we come before Your throne and worship You
By Your Spirit's power You now draw our hearts,
And we hear Your voice in triumph ringing clear . . .

Refrain: I am He that liveth, that liveth and was dead.
Behold I am alive for evermore!

To Reign or Not to Reign

There we see you stand, mighty risen Lord,
Clothed in garments pure and holy, shining bright.
Eyes of flashing fire, feet like burnished bronze,
And the sound of many waters is Your voice . . .

Refrain

Like the shining sun, in its noonday strength,
We now see the glory of Your wondrous face.
Once that face was marred, but now You're glorified,
And Your words like a two-edged sword have mighty power . . .

Refrain: I am He that liveth, that liveth and was dead.
Behold I am alive for evermore!

Stirring stuff. But what about the person who is hurting, or grieving or faced with crippling financial burdens? What about the person worn to a frazzle looking after a bedridden loved one demanding round-the-clock attention? When the going gets really tough and God doesn't seem to be around, what then? It is at times like that when doubt and unbelief really come to the surface. All that stirring stuff about Jesus and what He has accomplished for me! 'Is it really relevant in my situation?' They might very well ask.

NOTES:
[1] Isaiah 53:2b
[2] ibid.
[3] Matt 28:16,17
[4] Luke 24:13ff
[5] Luke 24:27
[6] Luke 24:31b,32
[7] Luke 24:37
[8] Luke 24:38
[9] Luke 24:36b
[10] Luke 24:39
[11] Luke 24:41

Resurrection: Fact or Fantasy?

[12] Luke 24: 41–43
[13] John 20:14–15
[14] John 20:15
[15] John 20:15
[16] John 20:16
[17] John 20:25
[18] John 20:26
[19] John 20:20a
[20] John 1:45–49
[21] John 20:28
[22] John 21:4
[23] John 21:5
[24] John 21:6
[25] See Luke 5:4–8
[26] John 21:12
[27] Isaiah 53:2
[28] Isaiah 52:14
[29] 2 Cor.5:21 (*KJV*)
[30] 1 Pet.2:24
[31] Mark 15:34 (*GNB* and *KJV*)
[32] Matt 8:17 (*RSV*)
[33] Rev. 1:10ff
[34] Heb.4:12ff
[35] Rev. 19:15
[36] Rev. 1:17f
[37] John 19:31
[38] John 19:33–35
[39] Thank You Music, copyright 1982

Chapter 6

MARTYRS AND TYRANTS?

There are times when we all have crosses to bear and, in weaker moments, fall prey to a spirit of defeat. Those are the times when doubt and unbelief can pull us down. When it happens, we focus on doubt or unbelief instead of turning to God. Satan delights in that. He beavers away at ensuring that doubt and unbelief remain at the top of our agenda. When he is successful in that, we question God's existence, question the relevance of what Christ has done, and question God's ability to do anything for us! We not only become slaves to doubt and unbelief, we sometimes give them permission to be the tyrants that hold our lives in bondage to failure.

People often say to us, 'It's all very well for you, God has done so much for you in your lives.' But we too have struggled with adverse circumstances and experienced those times when we have not been able to see the light at the end of the tunnel. And, yes, we continue to be challenged by them!

Scripture offers a solution. The secret, Paul reveals, is this: 'Be joyful always, pray at all times, *be thankful in all circumstances*. This is what God wants from you in your life in union with Christ Jesus'.[1] That's easy to do on our good days. Have you tried doing it when everything is against you? That's a very different story! Jill or I sometimes have to bring this to the attention of the other when one is 'in the dumps', or experiencing a 'downer'.

It is when we begin to praise God, that we have seen Him deal with apparently insurmountable difficulties. As a friend said in a letter: 'There is at times a deep sacrifice in praise. There are times when we must praise God though tears are in our eyes. There is power in praise. Make it a rule to thank and praise God for everything that happens to you, for it is certain that, whatever seeming calamity comes to you, if you thank and praise God for it, you turn it into a blessing. Complaining will drag you down into the darkness of despondency. Praise will lift you into the light of His presence. It is a lesson we all need to learn.'[2]

Paul frequently talks of the need for Christians to encourage one another. We have found it helpful to others when we have been open and shared some of the difficulties we faced after leaving our home in Zimbabwe – with virtually nothing – and starting a new life in the UK. Rather than speak philosophically about doubt and unbelief, and the power that God offers, it is important to do what Paul did: 'I can be proud of my service for God. I will be bold *and speak only about what Christ has done through me* . . . by means of words and deeds, by the power of miracles and wonders, and by the power of the Spirit of God'.[3]

One thing we have learnt is not to give up on prayer simply because we don't see the prayer answered as soon as we would like. God not only expects us to be patient, but persistent in prayer. When prayer for healing seems to produce no result, people sometimes give up. Some conclude they must be unworthy or unlovable in God's eyes. But sometimes we *do* have to wait. *His timing* will always be right. Our prayer in such circumstances must be a simple statement of belief in someone we know to be caring and loving: 'Lord, we don't understand; but we trust You.' Don't give up! Keep on seeking.

For a long time after arriving in England neither Diana or Lynne, our daughters, (nor Jill nor I for that matter) could watch filmed sequences of riots, or chanting mobs, or scenes of guerrilla warfare on television. Memories were still too vivid and they brought to mind events best forgotten. That is true of all traumatized or abused people. But all too often the events get buried deep in the subconscious.

Lynne, now at University, was certainly deeply traumatized by those events. She was just turning six as we arrived here in England to live

Martyrs and Tyrants?

and we found it strange that she seemed unable to remember places, or many of the people we knew, in Zimbabwe. When looking through old photographs, she wouldn't 'recognize' places, or people. When we were asked questions about the events that had taken place in Mutare, she would 'switch-off' and take no further part in the conversation, or deliberately leave the room. This continued for over two years despite ongoing prayer. Then quite suddenly she began talking quite normally about her home in Zimbabwe, taking out photograph albums and pointing to places and people she knew . . . the release brought about by healing within, and the new-found security in her UK surroundings.

Jill and I thought we had coped with such memories . . . but no!

For Jill, it was seeing the film *Wild Geese* (filmed in areas we know well around Messina and Tchipise Hot Springs in the Northern Transvaal) that tore her apart. It recalled the senseless and brutal killing of black and white, the hatred between various factions – black and black, black and white, white and white; the seeming hopelessness of bringing sense and sanity out of it all.

For me it was the events in Romania late in 1989, the brutal reign of terror and the events leading to Ceaucescu's downfall, that brought out feelings of anger and of betrayal buried deep within.

The story broke shortly before Christmas and concerned Laszlo Tokes, much loved pastor of Timisoara, who was victimized and persecuted by the secret police. The people had finally had enough. They came out in their thousands. The world heard only the briefest scraps of news before Ceaucescu sealed the borders and imposed a total news blackout. But other agencies spoke of a purge in Timisoara and of mass graves. Days later the Ceaucescu reign of terror ended. Gruesome TV pictures revealed both the carnage and Romania's appalling poverty, and set against that the grotesque expenditure on Ceaucescu's palace – built to eclipse all others.

Where was God, one might well ask, in all that misery and suffering under such a tyrannical regime? Yet there too, one discovered the miracle of God's ongoing work – despite the hell-hole they lived in – in people like Laszlo Tokes, his father, and the large and lively congregations they ministered to.

Someone once wrote: 'There is no sweeter music under heaven, there is no more fragrant perfume than that which arises from a life of suffering which is nevertheless filled with praise'.[4]

Laszlo Tokes, a courageous pastor, miraculously survived. His bishop connived with the state to try and evict him from the large charismatic church he served. Another bishop, at the state's behest, set about removing Laszlo's father as Deputy Bishop and Professor of Theology. When asked to deal with the son as well, he willingly obliged! On Ceaucescu's overthrow, both bishops resigned or fled.

All these events evoked painful memories for us on leaving our own home country. Despite much prayer for healing over several years, we recognised there was yet more repressed anger – perhaps unforgiveness too – needing attention.

We learnt much from such experiences, not least the time it takes to flush out the inner hurt and anger. Our healing has freed us to be used extensively in the healing ministry. A positive step, we learnt by experience, is the need to ask God's blessing on those who've hurt you! A *systematic* asking of God to bless them *each time* anger or hurt surfaces, leads to inner healing.

Clearly this is why Jesus said: '*Love* your enemies and *pray for* those who persecute you'.[5] Bottled up emotions are like a poison; they cripple and maim, rendering us less effective for God to use.

This is equally true of false shame and guilt especially for those who have been raped, or sexually or mentally abused. The false guilt or shame is often exacerbated by imagined, or spoken, accusations: 'You must have led them on, or flaunted your sexuality in front of them, or . . .' Often victims of abuse have no one with whom to share their pain. Why? Because they think members of the family, or friends, would reject them if their secret was discovered.

How easy it is to become slaves to fear, pain, hurt, victimization, false shame or guilt, or circumstance. In wonderful contrast is the relief people experience when healing takes place!

Scripture assures us that 'in all things God works for good with

Martyrs and Tyrants?

those who love Him, those whom He has called according to His purpose'.[6] It is important to see that well-known quotation in the context in which it is found: 'I consider that what we suffer . . . cannot be compared . . . with the glory . . . to be revealed . . . all of creation groans . . . it is not just creation alone which groans; we who have the Spirit as the first of God's gifts also groan . . .'[7]

It is in this situation that God's word is that 'in all things God works for good with those who love Him, those whom He has called according to His purpose.'[8] So, 'if God is for us, who can be against us? . . . We have complete victory through Him . . . nothing can separate us from His love"!'[9]

God wants us to be 'resurrected' – new beings in Christ, in good and wholesome relationships with others. Then, filled with that same power that raised Jesus from the dead, we can begin to be really effective for God. We need to believe it!

NOTES:
[1] 1 Thess. 5:16–18
[2] Orpheus Hove, National Director of Africa Enterprise, Harare in *Update* (October/December 1993)
[3] Romans 15:17b–19a
[4] Source unknown
[5] Matt. 5:44 (cf also Luke 6:27, Romans 12:14)
[6] Romans 8:28
[7] Excerpts from Romans 8:18–27
[8] Romans 8:28
[9] Excerpts from Romans 8:31ff

Chapter 7

PANIC ATTACKS?

It's hard to think of something that erodes one's self-worth more quickly than being unable to find employment. But what really tore me apart was going along every fortnight to sign up for the dole. For me, the hurt, embarrassment and pain, sense of failure and humiliation grew progressively worse. Standing in a queue, or talking to officials behind a counter, left me feeling guilty. It felt as if I was being branded as a 'lay-about', or pitied as a 'has-been', or 'too-old-at-fifty' to be of further use. I wanted to shout out, 'I've applied for several jobs since I was last here', or 'I've got as far as the last two being interviewed for a particular position but only just failed to get it'. So near, but I might as well not have bothered to try for all the good it did me!

As one month stretched to two, then three, four, five it became more and more difficult to prevent despair and hopelessness gaining a hold on me. Simply trying to keep a brave face on it in front of the family, or creating an assumed air of confidence that everything would soon be all right, took its toll. It certainly did nothing to build up my self-confidence. So many doubts came to the surface. And unbelief, too! More and more questioning as to where God was in all this. Had we heard Him aright?

We had arrived in England from Zimbabwe in July, 1986 feeling like missionaries. I had served as a priest in the Anglican Church there for over twenty-five years, the last twelve as Rector and Dean of St John's Cathedral in Mutare. We had been so sure at the time of God's leading and directing. Having lost virtually everything we possessed we had come here, in faith, believing this was where God wanted us to be.

But faced with a growing period of unemployment, we found ourselves asking: 'Did God really speak to us so clearly about His direction and provision for our lives?' Or had we been deluding ourselves?

We believed God *had* said a number of things to us through Scripture and prophecy, and all confirmed in various ways before leaving Zimbabwe. One of these was 'to return to the land of your fathers'[1]; and both families originally came from the UK. This word from Scripture was confirmed by others praying for us at the time.

That was all very well. How would we survive in a new country with less than £400 to our name, which was all that we were allowed to take out of the country? That was made more difficult because we believed God told us we were to spend a year just waiting on Him for spiritual renewal before obtaining another post. We had a family to provide for! How could we have a sabbatical in a country where we were not known, and without the wherewithal to provide food, drink, clothing, housing and all that a family needs?

Are some Biblical promises too far-fetched or impractical? If so, you will understand our reaction when faced with these seeming impossibilities. One often hears the quip, 'God helps those who help themselves' quoted as a proof text! Some believe it to be from the Bible. It is *not*, and the quotation is *contrary* to what the Bible teaches. Why? The Bible explicitly declares the need for all to recognise their *total dependence on God* for everything!

We believe God says: 'Do not be anxious about your life, what you shall eat or what you shall drink, nor about your body, what you shall put on . . . your Heavenly Father *knows* that you *need* them all. But *seek first* His kingdom and His righteousness; and *all* these things shall be yours as well . . . therefore do not be anxious about tomorrow . . .'[2]

We were fortunate. Ten years of guerrilla warfare, and then much strife during our last seven years in Zimbabwe under a totalitarian

Panic Attacks?

Marxist regime had taught us much. But the world has changed dramatically in recent years. The Berlin Wall, the Iron Curtain, have gone.

I can remember receiving a letter from Zimbabwean friends much used in intercessory prayer, who travel the world in obedience to God's call. We were amazed when we were told God was sending them to Moscow. They were to circle Red Square as they called on God to break the strongholds of communism! That was well over six months before there was any inkling of this powerful nation being 'opened up like a can of worms'. But they were obedient and did exactly as they were told. I can remember wondering at the time what the Russian guards (and secret police and informers who followed and closely observed every visitor in those days!) thought of their shouted prayers as they called on Jesus 'to break the strongholds of communism'?

The point to remember was the rapidity of the collapse once it started, like the proverbial pack of cards!

The years of warfare in Zimbabwe, and the Marxist-Leninist regime that followed, brought us an experience of God who does indeed answer believing prayer, and who does work miracles in seemingly impossible situations!

Even so, it is something else, isn't it, when one's own future livelihood and security are on the line? Nevertheless we acted in the belief we were to leave our homeland, and trusted God would honour His promises to take care of our future. So we sold most of our possessions, but sent, at the cost of 'an arm and a leg', a small selection of crockery, cutlery, bedding and linen to provide some basic needs when we found a home. We then purchased one-way tickets to England with some of the money we had, and gave away what we couldn't take out of the country.

On the eve of our departure from Zimbabwe, we received an offer we couldn't refuse. A small group of Christians living in Theydon Bois in Essex (people totally unknown to us) had heard of our tribulations through a mutual friend and had been praying for our safety. They believed God was telling them to provide everything we needed, for as long as we needed it! And that is what they did from the moment we arrived in England and were wonderfully cared for. We lived with Vincent and 'Jimmie' Wiffen in Theydon Bois for six months. Then a flat owned by Richard Salmon (he soon became a Christian, and later went to Bible College) was lent to us.

As *Rain in a Dry Land* went to the publishers early in 1987, I had mentioned the decision to try for employment with parachurch organisations. The consequence was I found myself ill at ease when I applied for such posts. The feeling resulted from an understanding that a full-time ministry for me, with my training, had to be more effective than a part-time one. *Rain in a Dry Land*, as far as questioning about my future ministry was concerned, ended with these words: 'Whether the door is opened for us to continue ministry in the Church of England, or whether God has some other full-time ministry in the wider Church, waits to be seen. We seek only to be obedient to God's will and purpose for our lives . . .'[3]

During the months following I applied for a number of posts. One of these was for the post of Team Rector in a Team ministry, and the reply I received inferred that only those with considerable experience as Team Vicars or Team Rectors in a team ministry would be eligible. I had not had that specific experience. So I ignored all advertisements for Team Rectors' posts on principle! How easy it is to be hurt by implied rejection!

Jill and I tried to buoy each other up by reminding ourselves of God's earlier promises to us. But one month followed another without any positive response.

Then, as with anyone out of work, we were so excited when I was accepted for a post as vicar of a parish. At the time it seems any job is better than nothing. This one was for two country villages in the heart of a beautifully forested and hilly part of the country – quite idyllic. When the Bishop suddenly reversed his decision, literally at the eleventh hour, we reached a low spiritual ebb.

However, with hindsight we realized I would have been a square peg in a round hole, and within a few weeks we bounced back. We all know the saying: 'When God closes one door, He opens another'. In the book of Revelation He reminds us of another way in which He sometimes works: when *God opens a door*, it will not be shut.[4] His timing, His purpose, is always perfect; so we deliberately set our minds to trust God afresh. Easy to say, so difficult to practice when nothing seems to be on offer.

And all the while those fortnightly visits to sign on for the dole did nothing to lessen my feeling of humiliation. It certainly increased my awareness of the deep scars many suffer through unemployment, a fear that eats into one's very soul, if one lets it do so. The fear of being unable to pay the gas or electricity bill and having it cut off, can result in severe deprivation for a family in winter, with consequent illness.

Then there is the sadness, the sense of unfairness, even injustice, that comes from not having anything to spare for a treat at Christmas, or a birthday, especially when children are deprived of the simple joy of presents.

Each failure to land a job at an interview slowly but surely whittles away any confidence or self-esteem there might have been. Eventually, chances of ever landing a job, with confidence and morale at such low ebb, become remote.

A particular humiliation occurs when the DHSS decides an alteration is necessary to the regular amount being paid, and the normal fortnightly cheque fails to arrive on due date. Having budgeted the previous fortnight's money to the last penny, suddenly there is literally no money in the house for anything. A long walk to the office to question the non-arrival of the payment gets the response: 'You'll have to wait until the computer has processed the changes and printed a new cheque; but don't worry, the cheque should be on its way to you in the next few days . . .'

'*Don't worry*'? How many times did I hear that being said to someone at the counter. There was no thought as to what a penniless family does for food while they wait. Imagine no money for the gas/electricity meter – so no heating or hot water. Sitting in a darkened house without light, unable to boil a kettle to make a comforting cup of tea, unable to cook the food that some kind person has left at the door.

Do those who prune overheads to satisfy shareholders and award themselves, as a *quid pro quo,* quite immorally vast bonus-related salaries think of the misery sometimes created for former employees?

A particular high spot for me during those months, so far as my relationship with social security was concerned, was when I walked in one week and told them my weekly payments would have to be reduced! 'Why?' they asked. 'I have just received a royalty cheque on the publication of my book *Rain in a Dry Land'*, I replied. The incredulity and amazement on the official's face when I told him I had actually had a book accepted for publication, and been paid for it, did so much to boost my morale!

But the continuing unemployment didn't seem to make any sense in the light of all the prophecies we believed God had given. We had now been close to a year without employment, and still there was no sign of a light at the end of the tunnel.

But just as suddenly everything changed. The post I finally obtained came, one might almost say, by accident! When the April list of Anglican vacancies arrived through the post, several offers seemed attractive. After praying about them for several days, I sent off applications for a couple of posts on offer, and left the list lying on my desk. A week later I noticed a vacancy that had been added as a 'PS' at the end – and so not in any of the specific job categories that I would look at. When I came across it, I was fascinated by the parish it described:

> Emmanuel Church Northampton, population 20,000. Shared Church. Local Ecumenical project has been extremely successful in creating a large and vigorous congregation in an area settled largely by unchurched immigrants from London. It has been a model of how ecumenical co-operation can power effective evangelical and missionary outreach . . . special skills and expertise are needed to help the congregation to establish the organisation and the administrative procedures needed for what is quite a complex operation . . . deeply satisfying post. Four bedroom

Panic Attacks?

vicarage. Apply . . .

'Now that,' I thought, 'is really right up my street.' All through the day a thrill of excitement ran through me as I thought about it. I made up my mind and wrote an application to the Archdeacon in time to catch the last post of the day. Only later that evening did I realise I had probably wasted my time, and experienced such disappointment. Why? Looking at the advertisement afresh, I saw something I had overlooked before: they were looking for a 'Team Rector', the category someone had previously told me was only for those who had team ministry experience!

So what greater surprise than to receive a phone call the next afternoon from Archdeacon Bazil Marsh thanking me for the application. He had already checked with one of my referees, Bishop Paul Burrough – a former bishop of mine in Zimbabwe, and well known to Bazil because he had recently retired from Peterborough Diocese. He asked me to attend a preliminary interview the following week, and to look at the parish. Within weeks I was to be accepted by the Diocesan Patronage Board, and my appointment approved by the Bishop.

We were to be reminded of two further promises we believe God had given us before leaving Zimbabwe. One of these was that God would 'restore the years locust had eaten'.[5] To us that implied God would replace all that we had lost. Several believed it not only had to do with material losses, but loss of position and responsibility as well. That was underlined for me through a prophecy given on a couple of occasions by different men of God: 'Your ministry will principally be with shepherds rather than sheep'. Under normal circumstances that was virtually impossible when one starts from scratch in a new country, and amongst clergy with their own 'pecking order', their own 'old-boy' networks. Yet within months of taking office, I was appointed Rural Dean of the Northampton Deanery! God's hand was certainly seen in all that followed.

NOTES:
[1] Genesis 48:21 (*KJV*)
[2] Matt. 6:25–34 (*RSV*)

[3] *Rain in a Dry Land* Page 220
[4] Rev. 3:8
[5] Joel 2:25

Chapter 8

GOD'S PROMISES FULFILLED

Yes, with hindsight, we *can* say that God's hand can be seen in so much that followed. But that does not mean, because God's hand was in it, that from that moment on He provided a bed of roses. Not at all. There were many times when things were difficult, frustrating, even impossible. There were times when nothing seemed to go right. There were doubts and question marks over God's purposes. Sometimes we wondered if He was still in the situation. Each time we would have to check out and discern where God was, and discover His path afresh.

When Jill and I arrived in Northampton at the Archdeacon's home, we had interesting and very diverse roles to play. Mine was to be interviewed by the Board, Jill's role has to be a classic in such circumstances. Audrey Marsh being away, Bazil asked Jill to act as hostess and get the meal! When the Board went upstairs to get their act together, Jill and I rolled up our sleeves and set out the food and drink in readiness for lunch.

It's not easy eating lunch socially with a group of strangers you know have privately dissected you during the past hour prior to the interview! However, after the interview I was told the Board were happy to appoint me as the new Team Rector of Emmanuel, and my appointment would shortly be confirmed when I met with the Bishop. What followed was God's amazing provision for us as a family.

We had made appointments for Monday 18th May to meet with carpeting firms at our new home in Northampton. On reviewing our financial situation at the weekend, in the flat in Debden, we realised we would be able to provide little other than the barest essentials especially where carpeting was concerned. However, in faith, we had already contacted those firms and asked them to advise us as to what was possible without borrowing money. In our prayers that Sunday night, the family committed our need to God.

We were getting into the car outside the flat in Debden the next morning, when the postman arrived and gave us our mail. Out of the blue, more than a thousand pounds in cheques fell out of those envelopes! We could scarcely contain our excitement and our wonder, as we gave thanks to God. We had a marvellous day; not too surprising, was it? We had our house carpeted wall-to-wall. We took it as a sign that the money, arriving as it did in answer to prayer literally moments before driving off, was for carpeting.

This turned out to be right. It was followed by a quite extraordinary string of events. Whoever described Mondays as 'blue'? During the next fortnight so much money came in through the post that we were assured of a home not only carpeted wall-to-wall, but also furnished throughout, and provided with all the essential, modern electrical gadgets needed to ease the burden of the modern housewife. For us, a miracle indeed! How we praised God for His provision, and for the generosity of so many.

But should we be surprised? We were sure God had previously made this promise to us in Zimbabwe when we were being uprooted: 'Therefore take no thought, saying, What shall we eat? or, What shall we drink? or, Wherewithal shall we be clothed? . . . seek ye first the kingdom of God, and His righteousness; and all these things shall be added unto you'.[1]

'Take no thought for your life'[2] from a worldly standpoint sounds like escapism. It is not. It is a Scriptural warning against the very natural dependency we place on our own efforts and abilities . . . 'We are never free from the recurring tides of this encroachment'[3] . . . whether it be clothes, food, money, friends, difficult circumstances (or lack of any of them) . . . When we hear the words 'Take no thought for your life' . . .

God's Promises Fulfilled

'common sense shouts loud and says "That's absurd, I *must* consider [them]'"[4] They are essential to my wellbeing, we say. But Jesus warns us *not* to let them dominate our thoughts for '(He) knows our circumstances better than we do, and He says we must not think about these things so as to make them the one concern of our life. Whenever there is competition, be sure that you put your relationship to God first'.[5]

We had done our best to take that promise to heart and were now seeing it wonderfully fulfilled.

Those were exciting weeks. We did something we had never done before – equipped a house with everything needed in less than a month! The timing was perfect. The house was as near ready for occupation as it could be, freeing us to get started with our new work by the time I took up my appointment. How bountiful our God is. Thank you, Lord, for Your amazing provision!

The exuberant praise and worship of my 'Institution and Induction' service at Emmanuel on 14th June 1987 will long be remembered, at least by us. A large contingent came from the Theydon Bois Christian Fellowship to form an interesting mix – a 'House Church' meeting together with members of mainstream churches!

Although such services are carefully devised to follow a formal pattern, I had, prior to the day, obtained the Bishop's permission to have an informal half-hour of praise and worship immediately before the service began. During that time it was our prayer that hearts and minds would be centred afresh on the living Christ – present and reigning in our midst – as we dedicated ourselves and our work to Him. There was an 'atmosphere' there, a sense of the living presence of Jesus!

However painful the disappointments; however endless (seemingly) the time spent *in limbo*, we could indeed look back with hindsight and see the hand of God in it all. That God brought us to Northampton has been confirmed many times.

It was confirmed at the outset by Bazil Marsh, the Archdeacon, when he received my application for Emmanuel. He mentioned to Jill at a later date that on reading my curriculum vitae for the first time, he felt 'a tingling at my fingertips because John's experiences matched so closely the kind of person we had been seeking'. The post had been advertised more than once before, but without success. With God, nothing is left to chance. His sense of timing, however impatient we get, however often we think *He* has forgotten or overlooked us, is always perfect.

How often we laugh at those poor fools, the prophets of Baal. 'You'll have to shout louder than that,' Elijah scoffed, 'to catch the attention of your God! Perhaps he is talking to someone, or is out sitting on the toilet, or maybe he is away on a trip, or is asleep and needs to be wakened!'[6]

Yet are we any different, in *our* relationship with the Living God, when we allow fear and anxiety and unbelief get the better of us? By succumbing in such moments, we fail to acknowledge the sovereignty of God in those very situations. Further, we are not to take things into our own hands. Instead, we are to remain faithful to Him and trust Him implicitly. As Jesus said, if you seek first God's kingdom and God's righteousness 'all these things shall be added unto you. Take therefore no thought for the morrow'[7] (that is, don't be anxious at all for anything!) . . . Easier said than done! How often do we actually pre-empt God's plan by our impatience, by taking decisions that satisfy our selfish desires and wishes?

We do it in any number of ways: choosing the area we live in; buying a home; selecting a job or profession; choosing a school; spending 'my' money; deciding on a church; choosing a marriage partner. How many Christians ignore the clear direction of Scripture that we 'be not yoked unequally with unbelievers'?[8]

Whenever we feel rushed off our feet it should bring home the fact that we must be doing things that are not on *God's agenda*, for He allots all the time needed to do the things *He* wants us to do!

In the marriage stakes, Samson's parents had a similar problem with their son. He said to his parents, 'There is a Philistine girl down at Timnah who has caught my attention. Get her for me; I want to marry her'. When his parents remonstrated with him for wanting to marry a pagan, his typically human, selfish reply was: 'She is the one I want you to get for me. I like her'.[9]

No. It's not easy waiting for *God's* plan, or for *God's* purpose(s) to unfold. But the waiting has to be eminently worth it. So began a new chapter in our lives . . . in England!

NOTES:
[1] Matt. 6:31,33 (*KJV*)
[2] Matt. 6:25 (*KJV*)
[3] Oswald Chambers in *My Utmost for His Highest* a Christian classic of daily readings, Jan. 27
[4] ibid.
[5] ibid.
[6] 1 Kings 18:27 (*Living Bible*)
[7] Matt. 6:31–34 (*KJV*)
[8] 2 Cor. 6:14 (*Modern Language Bible*)
[9] Judges 14:2–3

Chapter 9

TEAM SPIRIT: GROWTH OR COMPROMISE?

It doesn't take too much imagination to guess at the difficulties involved in getting a team of six ministers from four denominations working together closely on a day to day basis!

This was a fact of life at the Emmanuel Shared Church situated in the Weston Favell Shopping complex in Northampton where I had been appointed as the Anglican Team Rector in 1987. How do they agree on such things as acceptable practice, policies, and goals, let alone come to terms with the finer points of theology? The problem was compounded at Emmanuel because there was no overall leader. Leadership was by consensus!

Add to that the lay leaders of each of those denominations that have to be brought on board as well in the decision making process!

From a purely human standpoint such a decision-making process could be a sure-fire-recipe for a stagnating, indecisive organisation at best, or a disaster at worst.

Many will understand the levels of frustration this could and occasionally did produce; and what it might, and sometimes did to individual morale, and the consequent elimination of job satisfaction.

There is always the subtle temptation to give up the struggle and settle for a compromised or 'watered-down' Gospel, or to accept the lowest common denominator as the basis on which to operate, or to resign and move on? The greatest temptation of all, and the reason why so many team ministries actually fail, is to simply go one's own way, and 'blow the rest'!

To Reign or Not to Reign

It helps us to understand why most worldly organisations adopt pyramid structures. The Churches and Church governments have adopted these structures too. As in the world there are examples of power-hungry, even power-corrupted, individuals within the sheepfold.

Autocratic leadership is to be found in every stratum of the church, from the highest to the lowest, ministerial and lay. It is seen in the autocratic (or 'heavy-shepherding') church leaders – the 'you will do what I say' or 'what-Father-says-goes' type of leadership! It is especially true of some churchwardens, session clerks, church deacons and committee chairs. Indeed in leaders at every level of church life there are people who dominate and control, thereby exhibiting their own fears or inadequacies. They are a pain in the neck because power corrupts.

How common it is to find people hanging on to power well beyond their use-by date. This underscores their fear of being superseded, undervalues the gifts and abilities of others and results in the organization's stagnation. It sometimes results in the 'abused' taking their 'gifting' elsewhere.

Is it by chance that many bishops, for instance, have become more regal in their dress? They outdo royalty on occasions, and others have not been slow to comment on their outdated regalia. It puts them lightyears away from relating to most of our unchurched society. But an interesting and more direct pointer to that growing 'princely' status lies in a subtle change that has taken place in the last half century. It has to do with the colour of the cassocks and stocks ('long dresses' and 'shirt-fronts' to the uninitiated) that bishops wear.

When I was growing up and in the early days of my ministry, most bishops wore what is known as 'penitential' purple. In wearing it, bishops spoke of the symbolic importance of that colour. It was a timely reminder, some told me, of their own humanity with all its failings. More specifically, it drew attention to their servant role so graphically illustrated by Jesus in His 'foot-washing' illustration. That colour, almost universally, has changed to a 'princely' pink.

Power, or the means of control, we all too easily find ourselves striving for at every level, however well we try to disguise the fact and however consciously or unconsciously we go about it. It is found in every relationship: husband-wife, parent-child, employer-employee, director-board member etc. All, however subtly, jockey for position and power to take control and make decisions.

I loved the apocryphal story of a couple celebrating their diamond wedding anniversary. The local reporter asked them the secret of their success. The husband said that when they married they made an agreement. He would make all the big decisions that had to be made, and his wife all the little ones. The reporter, thinking he had discovered something momentous, asked the husband to give some examples of the decisions he had made. The husband replied, 'I'm not sure. I haven't made any yet!'

People not only jockey for control, but for status, better pay, and the perks and privileges of office. You name it they are all 'up for grabs' in the power game! Find me the saint who is never tempted in any of these areas. The Church is not exempt.

We are told that power corrupts, and absolute power corrupts absolutely. Of course that would never be true of you or me! If *we* had to go down that path, it would only be to create a *benevolent* dictatorship . . .

Surely the Church should be giving a lead in providing a *better system*, rather than emulating the worldly system? It is said the devil won one of his greatest strategic battles against the Church and its leadership when he persuaded it to adopt one-man ministries – the worldly pyramid system of power, the pattern seen in most churches today.

The result was devastating. Instead of every-member-ministry – 'a chosen race, a royal priesthood' – as Peter describes it, or *all* God's people trained and equipped to build up the body of Christ[2] – as Paul saw it, Satan successfully persuaded the Church to appoint more professional 'omnicompetent' ministers.

Subtle, isn't he! He picks on aspects of ministry we look upon as important assets – such as being professional, better trained, with improved skills and increased expertise, and thereby blinds us to his real purpose. The Church, in its wisdom, fell for it hook, line and sinker.

The result of the devil's carefully planned strategy, economical with the truth as he so cleverly always is, served two principal purposes:
i) The Church no longer made full use of the gifts, and the wide and varied experience available to the Church through its overall membership.
ii) Division – by a continuing 'worldly' struggle for position, authority and status amongst church leaders – was ensured.

The higher up the ladder one is, the more prestigious, powerful, and better rewarded the posts become.

The crowning glory, from Satan's perspective, was that from then on, most of the Church's one-man ministries would focus the bulk of their attention on:
i) Ministering to, and providing spiritual nourishment for, the pew-warmers already *within* the Church – instead of
ii) Equipping and mobilizing whole congregations to focus their many varied gifts, and the bulk of their attention, on those *outside* the church; that is, to the lost sheep who are Jesus' principal concern!

'Pyramid' systems of church government were not part of the experience of the New Testament. Some might contest such a statement. They would point to Peter and his appointment as 'the rock' on which Christ would build His Church. Surely, they would say, this points to his appointment as supreme ruler with Christ's final authority for His Church here on earth? Papal supremacy is based on that, and so too, to a large extent, is episcopal authority, or the authority in many churches, of the local minister or priest. And yet, is Peter the final or sole arbiter in the New Testament Church?

Clearly not in the story related to us in Acts 15. Both Peter and Paul are present at the meeting of the Council of Jerusalem. But after listening to Peter and Paul, it is James – as Chairman of the Jerusalem Council – who sums up the debate and recommends writing a letter to clarify the decisions *the Council* has made! His recommendations were the ones acted upon. The process they used points to a collegiate or shared

Team Spirit: Growth or Compromise?

leadership because 'the apostles and elders met together to consider this question'.[4]

Although people like Peter, Paul, James, and other Church leaders were recognised as leaders in their different fields, they still saw themselves as men under authority, and answerable to *one another*. So what were the New Testament patterns for Church leadership?

'Jesus called them all together and said, "you know that rulers of the heathen have power over them, and the leaders have complete authority. This, however, is *not* the way it shall be among you. If one of you wants to be great, he must be the servant of the rest; and if one of you wants to be first, he must be your slave – like the Son of Man, who did not come to be served, but to serve and give His life to redeem many people'.[5]

After Jesus had washed their feet He said: 'Do you understand what I have just done to you? You call me Teacher and Lord . . . I have washed your feet . . . [and] set an example for you so that you will do just what I have done for you . . . how happy you will be if you put it into practice . . .'[6] On another occasion, Jesus said, 'Whoever wants to be first must place himself last of all and be the servant of all.'[7]

Most of Jesus' ministry was carried on within a group; sometimes all twelve disciples/apostles (as trainees) were present; sometimes only one or two; on other occasions Peter, James and John. When the apostles, the disciples or the seventy were commissioned to go out and minister, Jesus sent them out in twos. It is rare indeed, if at all, that Jesus or those appointed by Him minister on their own.

Even after Pentecost those holding supposedly privileged ranks as apostles were most often seen working together in pairs or groups. The apostles themselves set an example. We hear of Peter and John[8]; Paul and Barnabas[9]; Paul, Barnabas and Mark[10] working together in leadership.

When Paul moved on from a newly established church, it was a group ministry that was left in place to continue the work his team had established.[11] His own team varied constantly in size and composition. He clearly saw such groupings both as the ideal model for training people in ministry, and for added strength – using the combined gifts of a group for ministry.

There is something else that is fundamentally important in such a system. No leader is left to work on his own. The support, encouragement, and spiritual gifts of each individual are there for the benefit of all. That is something seriously lacking in our one-man ministries, which by their very nature have broken many, and brought despair and discouragement to many others.

Oh yes! On occasions those teams fell out with one another: Paul, Barnabas and Mark are a case in point.[12] The Corinthian church too, reported on their leadership divisions.[13] Paul replied: 'each one of you says something different. One says, "I follow Paul"; another, "I follow Apollos"; another, "I follow Peter"; and another, "I follow Christ."'[14]

On her golden wedding a grandmother revealed the secret of her long and happy marriage. 'I chose ten of my husband's faults which, for the sake of our marriage, I would overlook'. When asked to name them she replied, 'To tell the truth I never actually made the list. But whenever my husband did something that really annoyed me, I said to myself, "Lucky for him that's one of the ten!"'[15]

One of the great joys at Emmanuel was the experience of working together, meeting together on a daily basis for communal prayer and sharing together of God's word. But there were also times when we experienced problems in working together. They had to be worked through, often painfully. Each time there was a change in the composition of the team, further dynamics were added and they too had to be resolved.

Many upsets and misunderstandings stemmed from a simple lack of communication; it could be as basic as assuming, or taking for granted, that the other person was aware of what was planned or decided!

'The Lord your God, who is present with you, tolerates no rivals.'[16] 'Where two or three come together in My name, I am there with them,'[17] said Jesus.

Some find that a problem! How *does* one hear what God is saying, or wants to say, in that situation? Yes! God may have spoken to Jesus, to the prophets and kings of old – but since then? Does He speak to us? For many the answer is 'No'! But: 'Jesus Christ is the same yesterday, today and for ever',[18] and God speaks, or wants to speak, to His people today just as much as He has ever done in the past.

If one is unable to believe
- God can and does intervene in our everyday affairs;
- In His personal involvement in our lives;
- He speaks to us in the here and now;
- He can work miracles in our lives . . .;

then what one is left with is a totally *impotent and irrelevant God!*

Further, Scripture clearly lays down how difficulties are to be handled amongst Christians:

'If you . . . remember that your brother has something against you . . . go at once and make peace . . .'[19] or

'If someone brings a lawsuit against you . . . settle the dispute with him while there is time, before you get to court'[20] or

'If your brother sins against you, go to him and show him his fault. But do it privately, just between yourselves. If he listens to you, you have won your brother back. *But* if he will not listen to you . . .'[21] then . . . 'take one or two other persons with you, so that "every accusation may be upheld by the testimony of two or more witnesses," as the Scripture says. And if he will not listen to them, then tell the whole thing to the church. Finally, if he will not listen to the church, treat him as though he were a pagan or a tax collector.'[22]

What is more: 'do not stay angry all day';[23] or, as the King James Bible has it, 'Let not the sun go down upon your wrath.'[24] Don't harbour grievances until a later date!

It's so easy to quote scripture! But for many, the process of raising the issue at the time can prove difficult. There may be too many strong emotions flying around for people to be able to cope with them. What is more, we are prone to putting two and two together and getting six. All too often, in our minds, we add a range of perceived slights or intentions that were never there in the first place. They result in making us needlessly more angry and aggrieved than we have a right to be!

Scripture recognises that. If unable to address the issue immediately, at least do not let *that day* pass without resolving it. The injunction 'let not the sun go down upon your wrath'[25] underlines that principle.

I remember hearing before I was married that there were two rules married couples should always observe:

i) Sleep in a double bed

ii) If you have a row, however aggrieved or unjustly treated you perceive yourself to be, do not go to sleep without dealing with the issue. Whatever it takes, don't 'hide' on the edge of your side of the bed all night. Before going to sleep, at least reach out a toe and touch your spouse's foot and say, 'I'm sorry'.

Sounds good and relatively easy advice to follow, doesn't it? It is – until you are so angry that there is no way you are going to make that first move! I've spent the odd miserable night in thirty-seven years of marriage because I wouldn't make the first move!

Any division that is not dealt with is like an open sore, gathering infection. For the team at Emmanuel to arrive at the point we did, took much effort and prayer. But with hindsight, it brought immense benefits and a church that really began to move forward.

NOTES:
[1] 1 Pet.2:9 (*RSV*)
[2] See Eph.4:12
[3] cf Gen. 3:4 etc.
[4] Acts 15:6
[5] Matt. 20:25–28
[6] John 13:12–17
[7] Mark 9:35
[8] Acts 3:1, 8:14 etc.
[9] Acts 13:1ff
[10] Acts 13:5, 13
[11] Note Acts 20:17ff
[12] Acts 15:37–40
[13] 1 Cor. 1:11–13
[14] 1 Cor. 1:12
[15] 'Heart of the Matter', Roderick McFarlane in the *Readers Digest*, January 1994.

Team Spirit: Growth or Compromise?

[16] Deut. 6:15
[17] Matt. 18:20
[18] Heb. 13:8
[19] Matt. 5:23, 24
[20] Matt. 5:25a
[21] Matt. 18:15, 16a
[22] Matt. 18:16b–17
[23] Eph. 4:26
[24] Eph. 4:26 (*KJV*)
[25] ibid.

Chapter 10

PRODUCTIVE CONFRONTATION!

After working for little more than two years at Emmanuel, I had reached the conclusion in my more pessimistic moments, that we weren't going anywhere; not only as a church, but particularly as a Team. So when we left on our summer vacation in 1989 I saw it as a time to adjust to that fact. However painful and unpalatable failure was, I needed to look to God for the way forward – perhaps elsewhere!

After our return I seemed to have instant confirmation of this. I received a completely unexpected call from a person in South Africa who 'found' me by a most circuitous route. A member of an Anglican parish, and former member of our Cathedral Parish in Mutare, had shared *Rain in a Dry Land* with fellow members of his church council. Their Rector had just been made a bishop. My name was suggested as their new Rector and, after praying about it, they decided to offer the post to me.

The offer was one I found hard to refuse. A large, lively, renewed parish in a sunny clime with miles of sandy beaches and the warm currents of the Indian Ocean nearby . . . ! What more could one wish for? The temptation to accept was considerable. After praying it through for a week, however, we decided it was not meant for us, however tempting.

It reminded me of the tale of the person who called at a vicarage. When he knocked, an excited child opened the door but explained neither priest nor wife were available. A telegram had arrived offering Dad a Bishopric . . . so . . . Dad was in his study praying for guidance .

. . and Mum was upstairs packing! The only difference in our story being *I was the one* almost set to pack my bags!

In our times of prayer I remembered the story of a good friend, David Richardson. He had held a very responsible position in personnel management when he felt God's call to work in Africa Enterprise, reaching the cities of Africa for Christ – with Michael Cassidy and Bishop Festo Kivengere. It would mean a considerable sacrifice, particularly financially, but he believed it to be right.

Yet on the eve of accepting, David was offered a prestigious public relations job at the top of the tree in his field. So, what was God saying; a door to Africa Enterprise; or the mission field into the boardrooms of big business? David believed God was showing him two things. Worldly success could be his; but was he willing to forgo that and accept a special commission from God? Faced with a similar choice, what would we have been tempted to do? David joined Africa Enterprise.

As I waited on God, I was reminded of all the promises we believed God had made to us in 1986, about coming to England, about His provision, about my role. We had, in remarkable ways, seen all those fulfilled. But now things were hard, was I just looking for a cushy alternative where everything was going well (the South African offer)? Could it be Satan's way of getting me 'to cut and run'? Or was I prepared to stay with, and work at, all the difficulties – and be where God wanted me to be?

As I thought about it, I did not think God would send us all the way back to Africa again when there was so much to do here in the place to which He had brought us. So I saw this 'tempting offer' from South Africa as God's way of asking me to look afresh at my situation; my disillusionment, frustration, and lack of progress from His viewpoint.

We turned down the kind offer made – South Africa was not to be for us. But should I look elsewhere in the UK? About that I was not so sure, and handed the problem back to God.

It is said there is no growth without pain. In trying to work together as a team there are times of frustration and disappointment; being let down and hurt; experiencing pain, even tears. Christian service is often

Productive Confrontation!

described in military terms:

> Build up your strength in union with the Lord and by means of His mighty power. Put on all the armour that God gives you, so that you will be able to stand up against the Devil's evil tricks. For we are not fighting against human beings but against the wicked spiritual forces in the heavenly world, the rulers, authorities, and cosmic powers of this dark age. So put on God's armour now! Then when the evil day comes, you will be able to resist the enemy's attacks; and after fighting to the end, you will still hold your ground . . .[1]

So what were the factors that had brought me to the point of thinking the time had come to move on? There was the important link which Team members had with their denominational hierarchy. There could be conflict because the latter would insist on denominational interests, priorities, regulations and requirements being a must. Those issues sometimes cut across Emmanuel's ecumenical priorities, needs and goals. For Team members that problem was heightened because it often resulted in their loyalty to denomination or Team – or both – being called into question.

It is almost unbelievable how time-consuming it is for an ecumenical church to obtain denominational approval for some project. Take a building project for example. Each denomination has its own forms, its own procedures, its own requirements, its own do's and don'ts. None take account of ecumenical structures, despite those constituent denominations having given their blessing to this ecumenical venture and given them a mandate for this.

Inevitably one denomination's processes required steps to be taken that another's rules expressly forbade – often on pain of losing out on grants that might otherwise have been available. I wasted hundreds of hours going through those frustrating, time-wasting processes, including travelling to denominational HQs as far apart as Manchester and Peterborough, to try and find acceptable solutions. But, yes, the end result made it worthwhile!

The greatest hindrance to progress at Emmanuel, the root problem we had to deal with, was the handling of the leadership problem. Any one person taking a lead on some issue, or making a decision – especially off-the-cuff decisions on day to day issues that appeared (to that person anyway) of no real consequence – could unwittingly enter a minefield.

The other side of the coin was the congregation's perception of a team that then seemed to be indecisive! This would often come about because a Team member had experienced just such a rap over the knuckles – so although the issue being questioned might seem simple and straightforward – no decision would be offered until protracted negotiations with all Team members had taken place. That too was not as easy as it sounds if one or two were away! What we had to work through was a way of affirming people's responsibilities in a variety of fields – without anyone feeling threatened or undermined as a co-leader by another.

St Paul underlines what results when this issue is not resolved:

'If the man who plays the bugle does not sound a clear call, who will prepare for battle?'[2] How much more uncertain if several buglers all give different calls? 'Let me put it this way: each one of you says something different. One says, "I follow Paul"; another, "I follow Apollos"; another, "I follow Peter" and another, "I follow Christ". Christ has been divided into groups!'[3]

In our case the danger could easily be: 'I follow John Knight'; or 'John Hawkins'; or 'Noel Beattie'; or 'Elizabeth Mayes; or 'Peter Goodlad'; or 'Peter Couch'; or 'Chris White'; or 'Andy Jowitt' or 'Margaret Johnson' . . .

St Paul continues:

When one of you says, "I follow Paul", and another, "I follow Apollos" aren't you acting like worldly people? After all, who is Apollos? And who is Paul? We are simply God's servants, by whom you were led to believe. Each one of us does the work which the Lord gave him to do: I sowed the seed, Apollos watered the plant, but it was God who made the plant to grow. The one who sows and the one who waters really do not matter . . . [that doesn't do too much for our ministerial ego, does it?] It is God who matters, because He makes the plants grow.[4]

Productive Confrontation!

Instead of avoiding the problems, it is important to be positive over the issues of confrontation. They are not always detrimental or unproductive. In handling confrontation positively, the first step is to swallow one's pride. Confrontation may result from a challenge to an interpretation of Scripture, or a teaching, or revelatory knowledge, or assurance of God's direction, or with what He wants us to do. Team members may well arrive at different conclusions over some of those issues.

There is also a need to recognise that the real issue to be addressed might be fear, or insecurity within me, or my church, or my denomination. How easy, on a given issue, to counter any challenge by saying, 'The Holy Spirit led me (or my church/my denomination) to this understanding' and presuppose the debate to be closed.

The danger is that it leads to the arrogant assumption, whether spoken or implied, that only I (we) have the Spirit! And so the '*others*', in coming to a different conclusion, must be misled. It is past belief how pig-headed or arrogant we can sometimes be. Whether we find it comfortable or not, others also have the Spirit of God . . . !

But what of *different* messages and answers that conflict? We have to take to heart the truth that no one individual, or group, or denomination has God's full revelation. St Paul understood that: 'What we see is now like a dim image in the mirror . . . what I know now is only partial . . .'

It's so easy when 'waiting on God' for individuals or groups to say of others, 'they've not heard God correctly.' and make snide remarks to others about the group one believed 'got it wrong'. That is often not true. What *is* more likely to be true, is that each individual or group has some *part* of the truth. What God then requires is for individuals or groups to pray together, talk it through with each other, and through that process discern God's fuller vision for the church or group as a whole.

It is worth repeating: No one person, or church, or denomination holds the key to God's full revelation. By handling confrontational issues correctly, God uses them to bring us through to fuller insights and understandings and to a deeper knowledge and understanding of God, and of His plans and purposes for us.

I discovered, with hindsight, an amazing fact. Although we couldn't always get our act together as leaders (sometimes appearing like a rudderless ship going nowhere) many people's lives were nevertheless being wonderfully touched and transformed by God! There is always the danger, because our eyes are so easily focused on what *we* are doing or failing to do, that we take our eyes off what *God* is doing in our midst!

Something else that brought much fruit through earlier power struggles was the acceptance that none of us were omnicompetent ministers able to be all things for all within our sphere of work. Over a period of time, and growing trust of one another, we were led to discern one another's specific giftings, and the importance of developing those for the benefit of God's work at Emmanuel and in the wider world. It was not for me, for instance, to find my position threatened in any way when an Anglican asked a team member of another denomination for ministry.

> It was He [Jesus] who gave gifts . . . He appointed some to be apostles, others to be prophets, others to be evangelists, others to be pastors and teachers. He did this to prepare all God's people for the work of Christian service, in order to build up the body of Christ.[6]
>
> By speaking the truth in a spirit of love, we must grow up in every way to Christ, who is the head. Under His control all the different parts of the body fit together, and the whole body is held together by every joint with which it is provided. So when each separate part works together as it should, the whole body grows and builds itself up through love.[7]

It is worth reflecting on Paul's glorious description of the Church:
> The 'body' itself is made up of 'many parts' we cannot do without the parts of the body that seem to be weaker; and those parts we

Productive Confrontation!

think aren't worth very much . . . we treat with special care . . . while the parts . . . which don't look very nice – are treated with special modesty. God Himself has put the body together in such a way as to give greater honour to those parts that need it.[8]

By early 1990, after much hard work at our relationships, we began to see real progress. Almost imperceptibly there were changes taking place in every area of ministry. Old and unworkable structures were replaced, unanimously approved by Council and Team, and new plans and goals were adopted. Importantly, many more people began to take a full and enthusiastic part in a whole range of ministries, and there was a growing excitement about where God was leading us as a congregation.

This was achieved, I believe, by a wave of systematic prayer on the part of a few committed people week in and week out over a considerable period of time. That prayer was born out of a sense of frustration over blockages and walls of division.

Suddenly, it seemed, some of the struggles for supremacy, both ministerial and lay, didn't seem so important any more. Appreciation and trust were more noticeable, and rivalries were not so marked. More people found their ministries affirmed.

On a lighter note, when the Team considered the Anglican team members (representing the state church? or because of superior numbers on the team?) were possibly riding a little cavalierly over the others, someone only had to say 'E.A.S.' (**E**ffortless **A**nglican **S**uperiority) to start everyone laughing!

What better time for us to have got our act together than at the beginning of the Decade of Evangelism? There was a unified purpose in seeking God's will, and then establishing a new congregation at Rectory Farm in time for Christmas 1993. And in working with the community at Boothville in the same year to enlarge the Community Hall and rebuild a further congregation there.

To be of one heart and mind is an important prerequisite for God's work to be carried out more effectively. Another prerequisite is the desire in people's hearts to build God's Kingdom – not our own. To die to self and be fully available and committed to doing it *His* way – not ours, nor for the consequent self-glory man often seeks. 'Seek first *His* Kingdom and *His* righteousness . . .'[9]

Jesus placed great importance on the need for unity. His High Priestly prayer at the end of the Last Supper says it all:

> I pray not only for them, but also for those who believe in Me because of their message. I pray that they may all be one. Father! May they be in Us, just as you are in Me and I am in You. May they be one, so that the world will believe . . .[10]

Every issue and conflict, real or assumed, that we worked through brought us closer together as a team. It brought with it a deeper love for one another, a recognition of each other's value and gifting; and a deeper commitment to one another.

Our own personal questioning about moving on elsewhere? It had gone! And then, isn't it just like God and His sense of humour to note what followed next? We had a repeat of our 1985/6 Mutare experience when God seemed to be asking whether we were willing to move on at His leading? But there was a difference this time. We shared with each other what we believed God was saying. Instead of thinking, 'Surely God wouldn't ask that of us now when everything is going so well, and we are so happy here', this time we were prepared to discuss it and pray it through together.

We both believed God was asking whether we were still prepared to move wherever He sent us. Were we fully submitted to His will and direction for us? Yes, Lord! But why now, Lord, just as everything is beginning to go right? The only response was, 'Are you available?' 'Yes, Lord.'

As we prayed it through together, the one thing we felt very sure about was that we were not to share it with anyone, nor were we to initiate the process by looking elsewhere. We were simply to wait until asked . . . !

Less than a fortnight later I was sitting reading in my study, minding my own business, not harming anyone, when the phone rang. It was an old friend, David Richardson, whom we had not seen for over ten years.

Productive Confrontation!

He was calling from Heathrow. Having said little more than 'Hello', and 'I'm between planes at Heathrow on my way from Vancouver to Johannesburg', he popped the question: 'Are you willing to consider moving to a new post?' I couldn't help but remember our response to God such a short time ago! So all I could say to David was, 'Yes'.

He then gave a brief thumbnail sketch of a large congregation in Vancouver that would shortly be looking for a new rector. He had already proposed my name as a candidate, and the wardens had agreed to David making the first tentative approach.

Naturally we were totally bowled over. To have such a clear request so soon after that time of prayer! And here was a congregation that had not experienced renewal, but was open to what God wanted for them in this area. But it took quite a while to adjust to the possibility of moving to another continent, and yet another culture. But if that was really what God wanted us to do, we knew He would undertake for us. Lord, not my will, but Yours . . .

I explained to David we were about to leave for the USA for the month of August, and gave him our address there in case someone wished to follow this up.

In our prayers, Jill and I said, 'Lord, You have brought us nearly halfway across the globe (south to north), and far from home and family; are You going to take us halfway round the globe from west to east and even further from home and family?' Still, we and the children agreed, that if that was where God wanted us, we were available.

Six months later I sent in a CV with my application at their request. But we were not chosen. In many ways it was a relief. The Team – they and my bishops were the only others let in on the secret when the application was made – were kindness itself. One or two laughingly quipped, 'John, you have to face it. You're too old to get another post. You're over the hill!' We all laughed.

But aren't we strange creatures? I took it as the joke it was intended to be. But a couple of months later while I was leading a week at the Green Pastures Healing Centre in Bournemouth, I discovered the quip 'you're over the hill' had really been getting to me! What if I *was* too

To Reign or Not to Reign

old to begin something else in my ministry? At fifty-six, was I past doing anything more worthwhile?

Fortunately I met with someone whose wise experience I greatly value, and he gave me much encouragement in this area, and a prophetic assurance that there was lots of life and ministry in the old stick yet.

At the end of 1993, twenty years after this ecumenical project was started, we had a specialist team sent in to evaluate the work and ministry at Emmanuel. They were very complimentary in their report: 'We want to say as loudly and clearly as we can that they (our denominations) should be very proud of this superb piece of local ecumenical mission. Archbishop Runcie . . . said, "Let local ecumenical projects be judged by their best examples". We say that this is one of them.' Speaking of the Team they said 'we were impressed by the commitment of the Ministerial Team, by their collaborative style of ministry, their keeping of a regular shared time of prayer, and by their forward looking. We felt it was good that they were working at shared team leadership, which is not always easy to handle, and sometimes runs the risk of things not being picked up or followed through'. As one can imagine, all at Emmanuel were greatly encouraged.

In my last few years at Emmanuel we had a really good working relationship. Like Paul, we could say of one another:

'I thank my God for you every time I think of you; and every time I pray for you all, I pray with joy because of the way in which you have helped me in the work of the gospel from the very first day until now.'[11]

After ten years at Emmanuel it was clear that if I wanted to move this was the time. If I didn't, I was unlikely to get another appointment since I would be in my 60s, and to remain would mean nineteen years at Emmanuel and outstaying my usefulness there. Bishop Paul Barber, in response to my approach on this subject, came back some months later with the suggestion I move to Greens Norton with responsibility for three churches at Greens Norton, Bradden and Litchborough.

This would be a totally new area of ministry, how could I know if it was right for me? Jill and I went to look at the buildings themselves. As we entered both the first and second church, Jill drew my attention

Productive Confrontation!

to the altar frontals – the beautifully embroidered cloth that hangs down in front of the altar or Lord's Table. The material used was a distinctive Italian brocade well known to us both. In 1961, thirty-five years before, my mother made a set of vestments for me, using the same brocade, for my ordination as a Priest!

Was this a sign for us? I continued to ask God to show me as clearly as He could that this was what He wanted me to do.

A few months later I was attending a special 'Pray for Revival' conference at Swanick in Derbyshire. On the last afternoon while we were all standing in prayer in the Conference Hall, an elderly lady in front of me who had never met or heard of me before turned round and said:

'John' (did she discover my name from reading my name tag?) 'God has given me a message for you.' In the Lord's words she reminded me that I had recently been asked to undertake a new work that would be quite different to anything I had done before. I was not to be anxious about it, as this was what God had planned for me. I was to know that God had already prepared the way for me, and I would simply reap what He was sowing. The message ended with the words: 'Don't be anxious or concerned because I go before you into Galilee', which I took as words of encouragement, just as they were to the disciples when Jesus left them. As she stopped talking, I realised lots of people were listening. I explained the details of my situation, and how wonderfully this prophecy had answered my prayers. There were many of us weeping together before God when we reflected on the significance of it all. You can imagine how excited I was when I returned home and shared this with everyone.

The promise of Jesus is that His power, the power which raised Him from the dead, is the power that is at work in us!

NOTES:
[1] Eph. 6:10–13
[2] 1 Cor. 14:8
[3] 1 Cor. 1:12,13
[4] 1 Cor. 3:4–7

To Reign or Not to Reign

5. 1 Cor. 13:12
6. Eph. 4:11–12
7. Eph. 4:15–16
8. 1 Cor. 12:12–26
9. Matt. 6:33 (*RSV*)
10. John 17:20–21
11. Phil. 1:3–5

Chapter 11

WHAT DREAMS ARE MADE OF

Well, what are your dreams made of? Love and happiness? A loving and close-knit family? The kind of job or career you really enjoy and which gives continuing satisfaction? Winning the Irish Sweepstake or the Football Pools or the Lottery? Material self-sufficiency? Idyllic holidays in far away places . . . ?

Did you know the Bible is full of God's wonderful promises that would fulfil many a wonderful dream. Our problem is taking those promises seriously, at face value; believing them, if you like. There is a stumbling block. They require the meeting of a prior condition if we are to reap the promise. The condition covers a principle that sticks in the craw. It is, from a human standpoint, over-the-top. 'That's impossible!', or 'ridiculous', or 'unbelievable' would be other ways of putting it. And because it is of that class, our natural human doubts not only surface, but often preclude any further action on our part. So we write off the promise as pie in the sky.

The promises of God involve the most basic things in life – like land, or money. Those very promises are passed over, or ridiculed, (yes, even by most Christians) simply because they are seen to be over-the-top. And the reason for this is that doubt and unbelief carry the day. It is these principles that we are going to tackle in the next few chapters. Perhaps you might start by asking God to take away any prejudice you might have. Ask Him to enable you to come with an open mind – allowing His Spirit to minister to your spirit . . .

To Reign or Not to Reign

The green issue, the concern for man's abuse of our planet and the need for a more careful use of its resources, has become very much the in-thing. God's prodding has something to do with that. He has always been concerned with our planet's rightful use and He gave that responsibility to us. There comes with that stirring of our conscience a deep awareness of the need to clean up, reconstruct or restore much of God's beautiful and wonderfully intricate creation. So much, to man's shame, has been destroyed already. So much more has been so abused, so thrown out of balance, so tampered with, that the chance of recovery is already questionable. Many are concerned, and rightly so.

The world's dustbowls are the net result of man's misuse of God-given resources. We've decimated the hedgerows, the flora and fauna; destroyed, or are well on the way to destroying, the forests, ecological systems, and the economies of most nations; we've polluted the rivers and oceans; created havoc with the habitat of virtually every form of life on the planet. All in the name of greed . . .

God has always been concerned for our planet, His creation. Way back in the time of Moses He gave clear instructions about the land. It was to lie fallow one year in seven. This would enable renewal and regeneration to take place. For nearly five hundred years the people of Israel took no notice. What amazing patience God had towards His disobedient people. Prophet after prophet warned that God would require a penalty to be paid for such flagrant disobedience.

The penalty was equally clear. They would lose their land and become captives in a foreign land. What is more, the punishment would be no more and no less than the number of years they had failed to keep the land fallow! God allowed 490 years to pass before He finally said enough was enough! For the 490 years' disobedience, the Jews would spend *one-seventh* of it – the neglected fallow years – in exile. Seventy years!

From the foregoing we can see it was no sudden, impetuous act on God's part. They had warnings aplenty. 'Don't say I haven't warned you!' He could say with justification. Five hundred years before God acted, Moses had prophesied the Jewish captivity and gave this as the reason for the exile.[1] We will return to this in a moment.

Nehemiah discovered God's patience and forbearance: 'They refused to obey . . . instead, they rebelled . . . But you are a God of forgiveness, always ready to pardon, gracious and merciful, slow to become angry, and full of love and mercy'.[2]

On reflection, many might think God was going to extremes in getting so hot under the collar about such a little matter as the neglect of the fallow years. Surely penalising them with seventy years' captivity was over-the-top! But if we think that, then we overlook a tremendous spiritual principle behind this whole issue. Starkly stated, the issue is this: Let go (let go of putting your trust in your own abilities and resources) and let God!

If we go back to the time when God first required the Jews to leave the land fallow every seventh year, He said this: "*When* you obey, the land will yield bumper crops and you can eat your fill in safety. But you will ask, "What shall we eat the seventh year, since we are not allowed to plant or harvest crops that year?" The answer is, "I will bless you with bumper crops the sixth year that will last until the crops of the eighth year are harvested!"[3]

The *real issue* God had with his people was not so much the failure to observe the fallow year, although that was important for the soil's restoration. Nor was it the fact that their greed led them to try and make yet more profit by planting crops in the fallow years. The real issue was their failure to trust God to provide sufficient food to tide them over the fallow year. A failure to trust in His Word!

They could not believe He would do as He promised: provide that bumper crop to carry them over two years. It is the area of faith most of us have a problem about believing! The problem of moving from the realm of the natural, the realm that sets store by our own abilities and resources, to the realm of the *super*natural. What God is looking for is childlike faith. To actually take God at His Word and believe it *is* possible!

In similar circumstances, the people in the wilderness were ordered to collect a double portion of manna and quail on the sixth day, so they would not have to work on the Sabbath.[4] On any other day when they tried to do that, the food went mouldy! In another instance Moses was told not to strike the rock with his rod the second time, but *to speak* to the rock.[5] He failed the test of faith: 'Because you did not have enough faith to acknowledge My holy power before the people [the very test church leaders fail their people in today?] you will not lead them into the land that I promised to give them'.[6]

One night I had a dream. It was so vivid and startling that on waking I remembered every detail, except one. It is rare for me to remember a dream, and dreams I do remember are usually startling. In this particular dream I cycled down a beautiful woodland path and somehow knew that I was going to meet someone. The dream gave no inkling of who that would be, or the why and wherefore of the meeting. I just knew that 'I knew', if you know what I mean. On reaching the edge of the wood, I dismounted and walked out into the open pushing the bicycle. (At that point in time I had not had a bicycle for thirty years!) As I looked ahead, the ground dropped away to a stream and I headed down in that general direction. Rounding a corner, I saw a beautiful Jaguar (the motorised variety) and 'knew' it to be my destination.

It was in a large open car park close to the stream; a typical beauty spot. No one else was around. As I drew closer, three car doors opened and three smartly dressed clergymen stepped out. They were dressed very properly (how incongruous, I thought, in such a beauty spot!) in black suits, with black stocks and clerical collars. But it was their posture that caught my attention. As they turned towards me, I realised why. They were carrying sub-machine guns! I continued to walk towards them. They found that threatening for some reason, and two of them moved off behind the car. The third stood his ground, but I discerned his increasing fear as I approached. At twenty feet his finger was on the trigger. The gun pointed directly at me! He was actually terrified of firing. I was no more than six feet away – and not a word had passed between us – when he pulled the trigger . . .

With that I awoke!

And the one thing I could not remember? Although vividly aware of who the clergymen were during the dream, I could not recollect one of them on waking! Was there some special significance to the dream? Perhaps the study I was doing at the time explains part of it.

For some months I had been mulling over a well-worn issue in Scripture. It concerns what often appears as God's Old Testament portrayal as someone vengeful, even bloodthirsty. Many stories seem to give us cameos of God that totally contradict everything we understand of the loving and merciful New Testament God.

> Then the Lord spoke to me, and I told the men who had been sent to me to tell Zedekiah [Judah's king] that the Lord, the God of Israel, had said, 'Zedekiah, I am going to defeat your army that is fighting against the King of Babylonia and his army. I will pile up your soldiers' weapons in the centre of the city. I will fight against you with all My might, My anger, My wrath, and My fury. I will kill everyone living in this city; people and animals alike will die of a terrible disease. But as for you, your officials, and the people who survive the war, the famine and the disease, I will let all of you be captured by King Nebuchadnezzar and by your enemies, who want to kill you. Nebuchadnezzar will put you to death. He will not spare any of you or show mercy or pity to any of you. I, the Lord, have spoken.'[7]

On the face of it, that doesn't speak of the God of justice, love and mercy *I* have experienced. No wonder many feel the need to cut out, ignore, or place less value on considerable sections of the Bible. Especially those, that on the face of it, seem to contradict what we believe and teach about God. Some have told me they even go so far as to actually ignore the Old Testament, and read only the New!

So it's not surprising really that people who are called upon to read such lessons in public worship find it difficult, if not impossible, to say 'This is the Word of the Lord' at the conclusion of that kind of reading. Of course, it is not only true of the Old Testament. Some find it difficult to declare some of Paul's writings as 'The Word of the Lord'!

To Reign or Not to Reign

For unbelievers and scoffers, how convenient to smugly quote such passages as an excuse for not believing in God! Frequently we hear 'the great and the good' on radio, television and the press trying to score points by gleefully quoting passages that would, at first sight, totally discredit a holy God.

We teach that this is the God whose greatest joy is to redeem and restore the lost, the fallen, and the downtrodden. We do not believe in a vengeful, vindictive, hateful or heartless God!

Yet the passage from Jeremiah, as with so many more in Scripture, would seem to provide good ammunition for those who would deny or mock the God of the Bible. What answer can we give to them?

We don't have to resort to any kind of cover up! There *is* a perfectly logical and acceptable answer! And it is one that vindicates the holy, just, loving, forgiving, and endlessly patient God we Christians believe in.

To be able to see it, we need to fully understand all the circumstances surrounding the particular quotation I gave from Jeremiah. And yes, we have to acknowledge that all the terrible things God said would happen to Zedekiah and his people *did* actually take place exactly as predicted.

But not for one moment do I believe God 'wished that' on those who were involved. Nor do I believe for a moment that the punishment was what God required as satisfaction or due payment for disobedience or lack of faith.

The opposite was true and the next few verses bear this out:
The Lord told me to say to the people, 'Listen! I, the Lord, am giving you a choice between the way that leads to life and the way that leads to death. Anyone who stays in the city will be killed in war, or by starvation, or disease. But, those who go out and surrender to the Babylonians, who are now attacking the city, will not be killed; they will at least escape with their lives. I have made up My mind not to spare this city [an inanimate symbol of their pride, a false god], but to destroy it. It will be given over to the King of Babylonia and he will burn it to the ground. I, the Lord, have spoken.'[8]

What Dreams Are Made Of

You see, despite their disobedience, God prepared a way of escape that would ensure people's lives were spared. They had to go out and surrender! Now that's *not* an easy choice. They might well be branded cowards, and worse.

Imagine losing one's honour and pride by surrendering before a shot was fired! Humanly speaking, it wasn't much of a choice! But God promised them this – their lives would be spared. The other side of the coin, as Jeremiah was quick to point out, is that their surrender would possibly result in their beautiful city not being destroyed: 'Submit to the King of Babylon and you will live! Why should this city become a pile of ruins?'[9] History records that those who surrendered were indeed spared, and taken into captivity.

But Jeremiah was the only prophet of the day who proclaimed that particular set of messages. All the others, the false prophets at the court, persuaded the King and his people to believe God was saying something quite different. They falsely proclaimed God would come to their aid if they stayed within the city and fought. What is more, they prophesied that by so doing, both they and their beautiful city would be saved!

Wouldn't that sound more acceptable? Who would follow a fatalist like Jeremiah? Whose message would we have responded to in such circumstances?

Yet God clearly foretold the consequences of staying in the city and not surrendering. The siege would be a long one with famine, disease and death resulting. When the city was finally taken, the conquering army would be so furious at being held up so long that nothing would be spared. Rape, pillage, and total destruction would follow. And the prisoners who were taken back as a spectacle to Babylon (not those who surrendered at the start) would be put to death as a grim warning to others. 'People will be shocked and terrified at what has happened to them. People will mock them and use their name as a curse. This will happen to them because they did not obey the message that I kept on sending to them through My servants the prophets. They refused to listen. All of you whom I sent into exile in Babylon, listen to what I, the Lord, say'.[10]

Note the battle that developed between Jeremiah and the other prophets. Some of the people *did* listen to Jeremiah and surrendered. To those who surrendered, the false prophets continued to feed them with false 'prophetic' advice. They tried to manipulate those already in captivity in Babylon. They ordered them *not* to build houses *or* to settle down in Babylon. They promised these exiles that within a couple of years the Jews would win the battle over Jerusalem and the exiles would return. The false prophets refused to believe the exile would last for seventy years.

Jeremiah, however, continued to be faithful. He sent those same captives a quite different set of instructions from God:

> Build houses and settle down. Plant gardens and eat what you grow in them. Marry and have children. Then let your children get married, so that they also may have children. You must increase in numbers, and not decrease. Work for the good of the cities where I have made you go as prisoners. Pray to Me on their behalf [!], *because if they are prosperous, you will be prosperous too*. I, the Lord, the God of Israel, warn you not to let yourselves be deceived by the prophets . . .[11]

Further, we need to note God made two further promises to those who voluntarily surrendered:

i) 'When Babylonia's seventy years are over, I will show My concern for you and keep My promise to bring you back home'.[12]

Striking, isn't it, to see what happened seventy years later: 'I [Daniel] was studying the sacred books and thinking about the seventy years that Jerusalem would be in ruins . . . and I prayed earnestly to the Lord God, pleading with Him, fasting, wearing sackcloth and sitting in ashes'.[13] God heard his prayer!

ii) God makes a further, far reaching promise: 'Listen to what I, the Lord Almighty, the God of Israel say about the treasures that are left in the Temple and in the royal palace at Jerusalem. They will be taken to Babylonia and will remain there *until I turn My attention to them*. Then I will bring them back and restore them to this place. I, the Lord, have spoken.'[14]

How often does one hear of victorious armies voluntarily restoring booty taken in war? Yet this is what happened here. The evidence for it, seventy years later, is found in the book of Ezra: 'Cyrus gave them back the bowls and cups that King Nebuchadnezzar had taken from the Temple in Jerusalem and had put in the temple of his gods. He handed them over to Mithredath, chief of the royal treasury, who made an inventory of them for Sheshbazzar, the governor of Judah as follows:

gold bowls for offering	30;	silver bowls for offering	1,000;
other bowls	29;	small gold bowls	30;
small silver bowls	410;	other utensils	1,000.

In all there were 5,400 gold and silver bowls and other articles which Sheshbazzar took with him when he and the other exiles went from Babylon to Jerusalem'.[15]

Now that is an extraordinary catalogue of events. We can summarise them as follows:

i) despite 490 years of disobedience, God had no wish to hurt or destroy His people: He simply ordered them to surrender to Babylon;

ii) the seventy-year exile would be their penance for disobedience in not allowing the land to lie fallow every seventh year; this involved:

iii) the neglect of the very important spiritual principle I have already touched on: to trust in God's promised provision for the seventh year;

iv) God would use the exile to rebuild their faith – as He had during their forty years in the wilderness;

v) Jeremiah heard God clearly and, despite persecution and every kind of vilification, proclaimed God's messages faithfully – in season and out of season;

vi) it was the false prophets, who refused to hear and obey, who were entirely to blame for the misery, death and destruction that followed. In a similar fashion, the cult leader Jones in Guiana bears the responsibility for a whole community taking poison, as do both David

Koresh and those who attacked the Branch Davidian cult at Waco in Texas when many people died in the fire on 19 April 1993.

A number of prophecies in recent years speak of unfaithful 'shepherds' or church leaders in every denomination. Clifford Hill, editor of *Prophecy Today*, believed God was telling him to put on an old clerical collar in the presence of an audience he was addressing. He removed it, tore it up, and delivered a message he believed was addressed to the Church of England:

> Thus says the Lord – 'As this collar has been removed and torn asunder, so I will remove you from your position in the life of this nation and tear you asunder unless you repent and return to Me. I am against you,' says the Lord, 'because you have misused your position of responsibility in the life of this nation. You have not faithfully proclaimed My Word, you have misused My Word, you have adulterated My Word, you have prostituted My Word. I am against you because you are unfaithful shepherds, and I will remove you unless you turn in repentance to Me and acknowledge your sinful ways . . . If you do, then . . . I will pour out My Spirit to cleanse you and heal your divisions. Then I will pour out My Spirit upon the nation to heal the land . . .'

Do these lend any kind of significance to my dream, and the submachine guns carried by those clergy? How many pastors are leading people to a spiritual, eternal death?

> . . . people will not listen to sound doctrine, but will follow their own desires and will collect for themselves more and more teachers who will tell them what they are itching to hear. They will turn away from listening to truth . . .[16]

Another interesting incident that seems to speak of a God committing mayhem is recorded in the book of Deuteronomy, almost at the end of the Jews' forty years in the wilderness. Only this time the roles were reversed . . .

> Then the Lord said to me, 'Look, I have made King Sihon and his land helpless before you; take his land and occupy it.' [And so] Sihon came out with all his men to fight us . . . We killed him, his sons, and all his men. At the same time we captured and destroyed every town, and put to death men, women, and children. We left no survivors. We took the livestock and plundered the towns.[17]

But there was no need for any to die. Going back a few verses, we hear: ' . . . the Lord said to us, "Now, start out and cross the River Arnon. I am placing in your power Sihon, the Amorite King of Heshbon, along with his land." '[18] And Israel's understanding of this message from God was abundantly clear when Moses 'sent messengers . . . to King Sihon . . . with the following offer of peace: "Let us pass through your country. We will go straight through . . . We will pay for the food we eat and water we drink. All we want to do is to pass through . . . until we cross the River Jordan." '[19]

So far so good! But the Amorites couldn't accept those assurances. Can we blame their natural human reaction? Who, in their right minds would want a migrating nation – perhaps two million strong (for scripture records over 600,000 *men* capable of bearing arms!) plus livestock – passing through the land!

God, on his part, clearly expected them to find a peaceful way. It went horribly wrong. The Amorites decided the only option was to fight. The Jews were so incensed they went berserk, killing and destroying everything in sight.

Like so many in every age, the Jews attributed their appalling actions to God!

God does not push us over the brink like that:

> Those who think they are standing firm had better be careful that they do not fall. Every test . . . is the kind that normally comes to people. God . . . will not allow you to be tested beyond your

To Reign or Not to Reign

power ... He will give you the strength to endure it, and so provide you with a way out [way of escape]'.[20]

God loves, cares, and does seek only to save. That *is* His nature. In love, He created. So His greatest delight and desire is to continue loving and caring for us individually, and showing mercy when we fail.

One night a man had a dream.
He dreamed he was walking along the beach with the Lord.
Across the sky flashed scenes from his life.
For each scene, he noticed two sets of footprints in the sand;
one belonging to him, and the other to the Lord.
When the last scene of his life flashed before him,
he looked back at the footprints in the sand.
He noticed that many times along the path of his life
there was only one set of footprints.
He also noticed that it happened
at the very lowest and saddest times in his life.
This really bothered him and he questioned the Lord about it.
'Lord, You said that once I decided to follow you,
You would walk with me all the way.
But I have noticed that during the most troublesome times
in my life there is only one set of footprints.
I don't understand why, when I needed You most,
You would leave me.'
The Lord replied,
'My precious, precious child, I love you
and I would never leave you.
During your times of trial and suffering,
when you see only one set of footprints in the sand,
it was then that I carried you.[21]

This is the God *I* have grown to understand, love and serve. The God who, from my own personal observations and experience, is endlessly patient with my shortcomings; who continually forgives; who delights to restore me to a right relationship with Himself. When I come across a passage that seems to describe Him as vengeful, unforgiving, or bloodthirsty, I sift through the evidence.

In the examples I've mentioned, there are clear and logical explanations to be found. But it is equally true that God, my loving Father, is prepared to discipline and chastise me if that is the only way to bring me to my senses when I continue to disobey Him. It is something infinitely worthwhile if it brings me back into line with God's will, and opens me up to all God has for me. Remember, each one of us is equally and infinitely precious to Him.

There is another factor linked with that truth that must not be overlooked. It has to do with what some would describe as a genocide God. It is quite clear from Scripture that God has judged His creation from time to time and found some people who merited His judgement. It was never a spur of the moment decision; He gave ample warning to people to change their ways. When they deliberately ignored Him, or continued behaving in a way totally repugnant to Him, He finally acted: so

He judged the world by water – at the time of Noah;

He judged the world by fire and brimstone – Sodom and Gomorrah;

He judged the world by an avenging angel – on the first-born in Egypt.

This is not our war. It is God's war. We cannot ignore the fact that God is God, and therefore He is also a God of Judgement. We understand, because He is a righteous judge, that those so judged merited His judgement. God is a God of love, and longs for all to be saved. But that does not mean we can wilfully trifle with Him. Think of Ananias and Sapphira![22]

Yes! There are so many areas in our lives where God expects us to have 'faith to believe'. The writer to the Hebrews understood what God tries to teach His people in every generation: 'To have faith is to be *sure* of the things we hope for, to be *certain* of the things we cannot see. It was by their faith [believing God and taking Him at His Word]

To Reign or Not to Reign

that people of ancient times won God's approval'[23] – 'for we walk by faith, and not by sight'[24] as Paul tells us.

Yet another facet of this living by faith is something we will look at next.

NOTES:
[1] Lev. 26:32–35
[2] Nehemiah 9:17 (*Living Bible*)
[3] Lev. 25:19–22 (*Living Bible*)
[4] Ex. 16:12–26
[5] Num. 20:7–11 (cf Ex 17:1–7)
[6] Num. 20:12
[7] Jer. 21:3–7
[8] Jer. 21:8–10
[9] Jer. 27:17
[10] Jer. 29:18–19
[11] Jer. 29:5–8
[12] Jer. 29:10
[13] Dan. 9:2–4
[14] Jer. 27:21–22
[15] Ezra 1:7–11 (See also Ezra 8:21–34)
[16] 2 Tim. 4:3–4
[17] Deut. 2:31–35
[18] Deut. 2:24b
[19] Deut. 2:26ff
[20] 1 Cor. 10:12–13 (*KJV; RSV*)
[21] *Footprints in the Sand* – Author unknown.
[22] Acts 5:1–11
[23] Heb. 11:1
[24] 2 Cor. 5:7 (*New American Standard Bible*)

Chapter 12

TELL IT LIKE IT IS!

I suppose every family has one of those days; moaning about the shortage of money, or the fact there is not enough to meet individual needs of the family. Or an unexpected bill arrives, and something special that has been planned has to be cancelled in the light of new economies being undertaken. Sometimes there are possible recriminations as to whose fault it was.

Looking back in time I have no idea of the detail that brought on 'one of those days' for us. It started in a fairly mild way over a number of issues, and began to fester (as these things so easily do when not dealt with straight away!) over a period of days. As so often happens, Jill and I both had very full programmes, so we never got down to discussing the issues that were niggling away. A barbed comment or two as we met briefly *en route* to the next pressing engagement only made matters worse.

But as we faced the issues on this particular morning, we agreed that our committed outgoings for the next month already exceeded our expected income. We still had the groceries to buy. The explosion came! It is to be noted these things often come to a head at the most inappropriate time.

So it was in this case, just at the very moment when I was dashing off to work. Lynne was also very upset, the unobserved and overlooked child 'in the middle'.

Strange, isn't it, the priorities we give to things in life? I had

To Reign or Not to Reign

appointments booked for most of the morning, so felt it right to leave a tearful and overwrought wife and child at home, rather than mess up my work commitments; commitments which often lead in my profession to offering good advice to others in distress! How often and how true this is of many who are used in counselling ministries. We overlook the Scriptural injunction that what comes first is good relationships at home – then we minister to others!

Yes, I had a miserable morning. I tried priding myself on the fact that despite everything that had happened, I was not neglecting anything on my programme, nor letting anyone down I had promised to see. We're great when it comes to the self-justification stakes! And yet, what a knot there was in my stomach about the hurt I'd left behind. But what about the hurt I felt I had sustained?

What, me let Jill and Lynne down? Where did that nasty back-hander come from? Then, in the true spirit of our selfish natures, we try to convince ourselves that ours was righteous anger; we had done everything possible – what any reasonable person could be expected to do. We only had the family's best interests at heart in the decisions that were taken. We convince ourselves our handling of the family finances was the epitome of selflessness. But a nasty thought pops into our minds. Was it really that selfless?

Well, there just isn't the money, and that's that! One can't be expected to get blood from a stone, or perform miracles every day.

Perhaps if I don't return home for a while longer . . . ? I cannot face all the aggro again! How can I carry out a loving, caring, compassionate ministry when things mess up like this? Maybe if I stay away long enough the problem will go away?

But I eventually came to my senses and realised I was no earthly good ministering to others' needs when my own home situation was tearing me apart . . . inside! I called it a day and headed home . . . It was true. We had yet again become so busy we scarcely ever had quality time together as a family.

Home at last! Brace yourself, kiddo . . . get it over with. Be gentle and understanding of all the frustrations . . . Just as I put the key in the door, it flies open. What a welcome! Lynne is in my arms telling me what a wonderful morning she and Mum had together . . . Jill telling me about a prayer time she and Lynne had shared, with God reminding them of so many blessings in our first year in Northampton. (That tells you how long ago this incident was!) They were so excited that they had done some artwork to illustrate how graciously and generously God had dealt with us . . . Lynne had drawn and coloured a beautiful card covered in floral designs with the following words:

>
> 1st June, 1988
> GOD HAS
> MADE US
> RICH
>

As we looked at the lovely card and thanked God afresh, there was time to ask forgiveness of one another; the joy in each face at setting everything to rights again. Then came the chart Jill and Lynne had drawn up to illustrate God's provision. There were so many things for us to wonder at and ponder over; each item bringing back happy memories:

ONE YEAR LATER

THE LORD HAD GIVEN US

A HOME WITH:
Carpets, Furniture, Stove
Washing Machine, Spin Dryer
Microwave, TV
Hi-fi
Amstrad Computer PCW 9512
New Car –
(Old 'jalopy' valued at £150 gets us £1,500 trade-in on special offer!)

SUCCESS IN:
Rain in a Dry Land –
Book of the Month 10/86
Work at Emmanuel
Preaching/Teaching all over UK
Appointed Rural Dean

JOY IN:
Many new friends
Scottish holiday with Andrew

ANDREW: (Son)
Overseas holiday in UK
Promotion at work
New friends in Zimbabwe

DIANA: (Daughter)
Success at College
Fees & Expenses met
Happy London Home/Friends
Car (From a friend)

LYNNE: (Daughter)
Happy at School/Friends
New Bicycle

MANY PEOPLE:
– learning about, and discovering a personal God who is real and active
– brought to the Lord
– filled with the Spirit
– received healing/wholeness in their lives

...AND SO MUCH MORE

We praised and thanked God together for the fulfilment of His promise to us while still in Zimbabwe 'to provide everything we needed'. We committed to Him afresh the needs we appeared to have for the coming month.

Tell It Like It Is!

Since the mid 1960s we have taken God at His Word. 'Put Me to the test,'[1] He says in the book of Malachi; 'give one tenth to Me of everything you have and I will open the windows of Heaven and supply all your needs!' It is our *needs* He talks about – not our wants! But supply them He will. That is His promise. Many have asked how we calculate the tithe. I believe it to be one tenth of one's gross income from all sources. I see it as the first commitment on our income each month; not something we pay from what we have left over.

I also believe it is to be given to the church where one worships. I have encouraged *churches* to give at least one tenth of their income to other Christian work and to charity. It has always been followed by amazing results – considerably increased church income.

But as this subject has been dealt with in great detail already in *Rain in a Dry Land*, I simply want to underline some things that will possibly help those who continue to question the principles of tithing and freewill offerings.

Personally we see our giving to charities as something over and above the tithe; what Scripture refers to as 'alms' or 'freewill offerings'.

Over the years we have discovered an amazing fact: the more generous we are in our giving – with tithes and offerings – *the more God gives us to handle on His behalf!*

No one can legislate for anyone else! However, we need to be aware Scripture has much to say about giving and tithing, and of our need to respond personally to those issues in obedience to God. What I believe God says to me through Scripture, and what you believe may differ. Certainly circumstances (as with a person who has an unbelieving spouse who is the breadwinner and holds the purse strings), obligations and commitments will differ. Clearly those factors are not unknown to God.

God expects us to respond with tithes and freewill offerings – but only with what is directly within our own control. For some it might only be their pocket money, or the cash they are given for housekeeping, or a clothing allowance, or money earned oneself. But every one of us can make a start with what we actually handle. If, as an unbeliever's wife, the only money you are able to call your own is £20 or £50 a month – start with that and give God His £2 or £5. God will honour that small beginning.

There are some simple guidelines to think over, and pray about, concerning this area of one's relationship to God:

i) God loves those who are *cheerful* givers[3] – not those who do it grudgingly, complainingly, or with a bad grace.

ii) The tithe, as I understand it, is *not* part of giving! That might be mind-blowing for some (or 'a red rag to a bull' to others) so let me hasten to explain.

iii) Everything we receive is God's gift to us, even what we earn, because our gifts and abilities are God-given. The Bible says we are to acknowledge this wonderful fact by *'returning to Him'*, as a thank you, one tenth of *what was His anyway*. (That's why it's not giving. It is simply returning what is rightfully His!)

iv) Abraham gave his tithe, or tenth, to Melchizedek, the priest of the Most High God. God's people were required to bring their tithes (the tenth) to the Temple.[5] Early Christians gave their tithes or initial gifts to the church. So we too give the tithe (the money we 'return to God') to the church where we worship, for the further development of God's work.

v) As many can afford to give more than a tithe – and the better off we are the greater the gift expected of us – so those gifts are ours to dispose of, as God leads and directs. When the need is desperate, even the very poor can give over and above the tithe – as did the people in Macedonia.[6]

vi) Jesus endorsed the giving of tithes – but expects further giving from us to meet the requirements of justice, love and mercy in a needy world, a world that cries out for just that from those who have so much more than others.

vii) We are *not* to give because of what we will get out of it. We give simply out of obedience, and with grateful hearts for God's generosity and the gift of eternal life. And, yes! God also promises to open the windows of heaven and pour out His abundant blessings. Having found us faithful in handling a little, He then delights to give us more – to be handled generously for His glory. The promise is not to pour out in abundance in order to make me rich. His promise is that we will need for nothing.

viii) Occasionally people have got into debt and blamed it on tithing, or suggested Scriptural promises on God's provision cannot be trusted because they got into debt by tithing. To put it another way, they ask why God has not opened the windows of heaven and poured out His abundance to keep them out of debt?!

It's important to note that those who tithe are as obliged to live within their means as anyone else. They should not take on increased mortgages, or car loans, or extra expenses presently beyond their means with a veiled message to God: 'As I'm tithing, I'm sure You will provide!' Having decided to honour God by tithing, our income and expenditure need to be brought before God constantly for His direction.

Banks and financial institutions bombard us with loan suggestions – 'Why wait, when you can have it now and enjoy it,' they say. They prefer you to overlook the fact that it will cost you a great deal more than if you saved for it and paid cash. Many find that credit card use can run up debts that soon get out of control. What is required of us here is to be as 'wise as serpents, and harmless as doves'.[8]

So, why had we run into trouble financially? A couple of unexpected car bills! Within a couple of days we received a refund we had overlooked, and then received an unexpected gift. Having tithed that, there was more than enough to buy those groceries needed for the month. 'We can trust God to keep His promise . . .'[9]. But we cannot expect that response to His promise unless and until we believe in it and actually take that step of faith and start tithing everything . . . and handling all our resources in a way that is honouring to Him.

The principle is just as true for those with very little to call their own. It is true for those on old age pensions; and it is true for those on social security benefits or welfare, as a number of people in our congregation at Emmanuel discovered to be true.

I was asked on one occasion to give some teaching on the principle of tithing to our Deanery Synod. At the last moment I asked a Methodist member of our congregation, Ethel Brand, if she would be willing to

To Reign or Not to Reign

share her testimony on tithing – but didn't tell her where! When I arrived to pick her up, I was wearing a suit. This was not something they often saw on me at Emmanuel, being more used to seeing me in shorts and open-neck shirts. So she immediately sensed this was an important occasion, and asked with some trepidation where we were going. I didn't tell her until we were well on our way! She and her husband Charlie had recently celebrated their Golden Wedding: and Charlie, sixty years as a Methodist Lay Preacher. Charlie had worked on a farm for most of his life, so they never had very much. But little though they've had, they have tithed their income throughout their married life, and Ethel gave instances of amazing ways God always provided for special needs or occasions.

Ethel told Synod members of her involvement with a church in Lincolnshire. Wanting to be of help, she offered to be on the hostess tea rota for the regular midweek gathering. When her turn came round, she was horrified to discover she was expected to bake the refreshments for upwards of fifty people out of her own pocket. With Charlie as a farm hand, and a young family, she couldn't afford it, in fact they had no spare money at all. All through the week she tried to pluck up courage and say it was just impossible, simply because she didn't have the food or money.

Finally, while cleaning out the hearth one morning she said to herself, 'I can't provide for all those people, I'll just have to go and tell the organiser.' She thought she heard a voice say, 'Use the money!' 'But the only money is the money upstairs we're saving for Mary's shoes. She needs those.' 'Use it.' 'But . . .' 'I thought you said I could have all you've got?' . . . Believing God wanted her to trust Him for this, she went and bought the groceries with the shoe money, and provided the church group with their tea. 'Next morning,' said Ethel, 'a lady came round knowing nothing of what had taken place, and offered us a new pair of shoes she had bought for her own daughter, but found they didn't fit properly. They fitted Mary perfectly!'

Ethel's story reminded me of the story of the widow of Zarephath during a terrible drought. Ravens had fed Elijah until the brook dried up, and then he met the widow as she was gathering sticks. He asked for bread. The widow told him she only had a handful of meal and a drop of olive-oil, and was collecting firewood to bake a last loaf for herself and her son. 'Don't worry', Elijah said . . . 'first make a small loaf for me' (she could be forgiven for thinking this was the local 'con' man) and then you will find your meal and oil will not run out until the rains come! Amazingly she took him at his word and did as she was asked! She and her son were provided for thereafter.[10]

On another occasion Ethel said to herself one evening, 'I really do need a winter coat, but I can't afford one.' Next day a lady came to her and said, 'You need a winter coat!' (Not 'would you like . . . ?' or 'could you do with . . . ?') and gave her one. It lasted her for years.

Ethel's testimony at the Synod really made people sit up and take note. Charlie tells of an occasion when a man said to him, 'I can't afford to tithe!' He replied, 'We can't afford *not* to tithe!' For over fifty years they have tithed – on a farm hand's wages, on a caretaker's wages, and now on their state pensions. As they would tell you, 'We need for nothing, and we never have! God has been so good to us!' You only had to see their faces and their openly proclaimed love for the Lord week by week at Emmanuel, and you knew that here was a remarkable witness to what God had done in and through two people's lives.

It was something very special to meet with a growing number of people in that congregation who started to tithe, and experienced God actively at work in their lives in ways they would not have believed possible a year or two before. A common phrase was 'It works!' Should we be surprised?

Two years after I arrived at Emmanuel, the church began to practise the principle of tithing. At least one tenth of all income was given away. Church income increased very significantly in the years we were there:

e.g.	1987	£29,193
	1989	£46,236
	1991	£59,526
	1993	£75,476
	1996 over	£100,000.

To Reign or Not to Reign

After ten years at Emmanuel, I became Priest in Charge of Greens Norton, Litchborough and Bradden in September 1997. All three of these delightful village parishes in the South Northamptonshire countryside had considerable difficulties meeting their financial commitments, and were dependent on all manner of fund-raising events to try and balance the books.

On my second Sunday in office, Jill asked me what I was going to preach about in the three churches that day. 'Tithing', I said. 'Well, that will empty the churches before you have even started,' she said and tried to persuade me that she did not think that was a very good idea.

In each church I explained the principles of tithing. I also said the major concern in all three churches was the burden of trying to pay the parish share. The total share for the three churches together was about £18,000. Because, I said, we as a family tithed everything, we would be contributing one tenth of this bill. All I needed was another nine people with similar incomes to do the same and the parish share would be paid. Another ten people giving on the same basis would more than cover all the other expenses, and after that we would just have money to give away! I also said that as a policy, the church would also be giving away 10 per cent (a tithe) of all its income to needy causes.

In just over two years the largest parish has not only increased its giving to such an extent that it has met all its expenses, but given away over £7,000 over two years (just over 10 per cent). We are now into our third year and have made another decision for this year – no major fund-raising events will be held this year as direct giving more than covers all commitments. Many have increased their giving, and the congregation has grown (not frightened away by the challenges given on tithing!). So far only a few people actually tithe. The potential for expansion is mind blowing!

As a family we had an amazing experience in July 1991. Diana had just let us know that her wedding was to be in Zimbabwe in the following January. We already had our tickets (non-refundable) to fly to the USA for an exchange of parishes for the month of August, so we had spent all our reserves. Andrew and Jenny, our son and daughter-in-law, had been married the year before in Zimbabwe – by me – and come to live near us. So they had no savings!

On phoning our friendly 'bucket-shop' (providers of cutprice airfares), we were told the five tickets would cost over £2,000! In addition, to ensure seats – immediately after the Christmas peak period – would necessitate purchasing them by the end of July. That gave us ten days to raise the cash. The five of us met for prayer on Sunday night and laid the problem before God. If it was His will that we should be at the wedding, then we needed this money by Monday week. After our time in prayer Jenny said, 'I've trusted God for all sorts of things and found Him faithful – but don't you think that over £2,000 in a week is stretching things a little?'. No one was told of our needs or our prayers. It was a matter between God and us.

Monday, Tuesday, Wednesday, Thursday, Friday came and went. No response! Nerves became frayed. We found ourselves getting short with one another. Obviously we wanted to be at our daughter's wedding! Daily we had to renew our trust in God and confess our doubts and also to be willing to accept God's will, whatever that was!

On Saturday morning the first letter I opened started with 'God has laid it on my heart to send you this money' – it was enough for an air fare! The second letter enclosed a royalty cheque – another air fare plus! (The previous year *Rain in a Dry Land* had been translated into Norwegian, and this was my first payment – something I had forgotten about) But what timing! We immediately phoned Andrew and Jenny. They too had good news. On leaving work the night before both had been given unexpected bonuses – and Saturday's post had brought a surprise tax refund. Together they were enough to pay their fares!

But there was more to come. On Monday I phoned the bucket shop to say we had raised the money. However the lady on the line said – 'I'm sorry sir, but the airfares were increased on Friday'. I said, 'You can't do that! You told us the amount we needed. We prayed together as a family a week ago, and God has provided exactly that amount!' – and filled her in on the detail! There was a stunned silence at the other

To Reign or Not to Reign

end of the line. I don't suppose she had had too many experiences of that kind. Eventually she said, 'I'll have to talk to the directors and get back to you'!

Half an hour later she phoned to say they had five tickets at the old price which we could have if we paid cash today. I said, 'Done'! Then Jill put a spanner in the works. She said we had agreed she could fly out a little earlier, which meant straight after Christmas so she could help Diana with last minute preparations. I said, 'You can't. If you fly before us, there is an extra premium of £200 a ticket during the Christmas peak. We haven't got that £200'. Jill was very upset and went off in some distress to help at the Church Coffee Bar. That upset Lynne and me. As we talked about it, we felt that perhaps we ought to have a little more faith. What was another £200 in the light of what God had already provided? So we phoned our friendly lady in the bucket shop and asked if she would change one ticket for this earlier date. 'But that will cost you another £200 and you said you didn't have any more cash'. I explained the circumstances, and said we would trust God to provide the extra £200! So somewhat reluctantly she said she would see if there was a vacant seat available.

She eventually phoned while we were sitting down to lunch, and told us she had found a seat for Jill on an earlier flight. But she impressed on us that the firm would only supply these tickets on the agreed basis if we paid for them in full before the end of the day. I said we would continue praying for the extra £200. I returned to the family with the good news and reminded them of the need for more prayer. Jill, naturally, was elated. We prayed right away, and then finished our lunch.

As we began to wash up, the phone rang. I went through to my study to answer it, and saw an envelope had been dropped through the door – obviously during lunch. When I opened it, it was a Building Society cheque for £200 – put through the door as an anonymous 'gift'!

Yes, some might say it was just a series of coincidences. But what a sequence! What timing! To us, it was a God-incidence.

Jesus talked more about money and giving than about any other subject. He did so intentionally. He was not embarrassed at drawing attention to people's giving. The reason for this is that money, and its control, is the *one* area in our lives we find hardest to surrender to God. That is why the only answer Jesus could give to the rich young ruler wanting to enter heaven was 'Go and sell all you have and give the money to the poor, and you will have riches in heaven; then come and follow Me".[11] You see he wanted to serve God – but in his way, on his terms.

Have you heard God speaking to you? There is no escaping Him when He does, because He speaks in the language you know best; not so much through your ears, but through your circumstances!

You see, when Jesus said it was 'much harder for a rich person to enter the Kingdom of God than for a camel to go through the eye of a needle',[12] he spoke of something we need to hear and understand. I can actually persecute, or ignore Jesus, by insisting on serving Him my way. Like the rich young man, I can express my desire to love and serve God, but insist on fixing the ground rules (e.g how *I* handle *my* money!). Jesus rebukes that, because 'ye know not what manner of spirit ye are of'[13] or, as He had to say to Peter, 'Get thee behind Me, Satan: thou art an offence unto Me: for thou savourest not the things that be of God, but those that be of men.'[14]

Jesus *sat* and watched people pouring money into the Temple coffers ... 'this poor widow', He said, 'put more in than all the others; [they] put in what they had to spare of their riches ... but she ... gave all she had to live on'![15]

Throughout the first twenty-five years of my ministry outside the UK, we received regular 'penny lectures' from Western Church leaders. The gist of these was always much the same: Third World churches must learn to stand on their own feet and become self-supporting. It is important to stop expecting, or seeking, aid. And they were sensible arguments! It's never healthy for one party to be always giving, and the other receiving. It leads to unhealthy relations – paternalism, subservience, authoritarianism, fear of speaking the truth, strait-jacketing ... And the worst possible scenario is to be always dependent on others. A church that is so will stagnate and lose self-respect.

Equally importantly, its members will not be encouraged to develop proper levels of stewardship; there will always be the 'cop out' and the expectation of someone else 'picking up the tab'. It seemed all such good, sound advice. But in all those cases, I've since discovered, it was the pot calling the kettle black! It was only after becoming involved in the system over here in the UK that I realised how hypocritical those statements were.

At a Peterborough Diocesan Synod some years ago, it was said: 'Since this Diocese is blessed with continuing income from historical resources, parishes are asked to pay only 24 per cent of the cost of clergy stipends". The balance of 76 per cent, was met from past historical resources; from benefactors in the past.

Within a couple of years there were angry protests from many parishes because the percentage to be raised by parishes – in our generation – had increased to 39 per cent! Increasing pension costs, stock market losses, *et al* had decreased the amount the church commissioners could inject into today's costs of stipends from their historic investments.

But they still had nothing to gripe about. They still raised scarcely a penny towards pensions, costs of parsonages, provision of bishops – together with their cars and expenses – and so much more; and not forgetting the hefty slice towards clergy stipends. All this from historic resources!

At the beginning of the 1990s, the average church member still paid less than half the cost of 'the 1990s church'. Since then the Church has had to look to its members to meet a far greater portion of all the costs, including a new pension scheme for clergy. Here we are at the start of the twenty-first century and the Church still relies for some part of its expenditure *on past historic resources.* Quite simply put, if those resources dried up, the Church would realise that all bishops, archdeacons, deans – and their expenses as well – could not be paid. Nor would there be any money for all those already on pension, or likely to draw a pension or more than a part of their pension, in the next few years.

Tell It Like It Is!

But many Third World churches *have to be* totally self-supporting in order to survive. Western churches – particularly the ones best known to me, the Church of England and the Episcopal Church of the USA, had the cheek to demand of others what they were certainly not able to achieve themselves.

Most churches and denominations in the UK and Western Europe cannot afford a revival! They are all into mothballing and closing of churches – and reductions of people in full-time ministry. Overall numbers of people in ministry have declined drastically because the churches say they can't afford to continue at this level.

Just think about these amazing facts: the UK population since 1850 has multiplied three-fold; in that time, C. of E. clergy have decreased by a third.

In 1851, 14,500 clergy served a population of 17 million people.

By 1990, less than 10,000 clergy served 50 million people.

That means the 1 clergyman for 1,172 people in 1851 deteriorated to 1 person in full-time ministry for 5,000 people in 1993!

For more than a century, the church has devoted itself to desperately defending what it has left, and still decreasing, rather than mobilising for mission.

Yes, a church that sponges off others, our forebears included, will stagnate, lose its respect and always expect others to 'pick up the tab'. I can imagine what Jesus would say of a church that utilises past resources in a way that encourages miserly giving today!

'Woe to you, ministers and teachers of the Gospel, bishops, superintendents, general secretaries, ministers! Hypocrites! You weaken and endanger the church's cutting edge by soft-pedalling the people's need to give sacrificially . . . !' To speak plainly, we are cheating God! And the church refuses to grasp this fact. It sees proper Biblical levels of giving, namely tithes and freewill offerings, as a nettle too uncomfortable to grasp. It fails to recognise, in so doing, that it has therefore denied amazing blessings to both individuals and churches alike.

What is so tragic is that 'they' (the shepherds of the flock) have done their members an enormous disservice. By soft-pedalling proper levels of giving, they thought to save themselves from antagonising members. Instead, they have actually robbed people of their proper inheritance; they have denied most of God's people the amazing joy of experiencing His abundant provision in response to obedience to His Word and promises.

The real reason for this failure is that they have not tried it for themselves, and they have refused to believe the truth of its Biblical and God-given principles. They have literally become what Jesus calls 'the blind leaders of the blind'.[16]

Jesus has particularly harsh things to say to ministers and teachers who ought to know better: 'How terrible for you, blind guides!'[17] and 'How terrible for you, teachers ... hypocrites! You lock the door to the Kingdom of heaven in people's faces, and you yourselves don't go in, nor do you allow in those who are trying to enter!'[18]

'Put Me to the test [tithe everything you have] and you will see that I will open the windows of heaven and pour out on you in abundance all kind of good things'.[19]

Gideon was allowed to prove God, or put him to the test, by laying out a fleece. In the same way, God invites us to prove or test what He says about tithes. Yet most church leaders won't even *try* it. They will spend hours theologising, arguing, considering every possible angle of what might be a *reasonable* basis for giving. However gently they are brought back to God's Word, however often they are encouraged to at least *try* tithing, they back off and defend their own suggestions for giving. They say tithing is unreasonable; they couldn't afford to tithe; they argue that the principle no longer applies in our twentieth century world because we now pay taxes and national insurance contributions.

They forget the Jews in Jesus' day would have paid 30 per cent and more of their income in tithes and taxes. Trying to trap Jesus they said 'Tell us, then, what do you think? Is it against our Law to pay taxes to the Roman Emperor, or not? ' ... Jesus said to them, '... pay the Emperor *what belongs to the Emperor*, and *pay God what belongs to God.*'!'[20]

Tell It Like It Is!

You name it, there will be an excuse for not trying it. But the problem is not going to go away. God will go on challenging, you can be sure of that!

Our Diocese, like so many churches in the UK at present, is facing a financial crisis. All sorts of things are being attempted to improve our income. A few years ago the bishops, archdeacons and dean for instance, were asked to publicly declare their level of giving to the work of God in order to challenge the church as a whole.

We didn't get much information on that except to say the Bishop was giving 5 per cent of his free income (after deduction of tax) to the church. Then rural deans made their declaration in order to challenge the clergy, and then the clergy to challenge the laity – hopefully encouraging all to give proportionately better than they had been doing.

I don't know what many of those figures were, but as a rural dean at that time, I had to declare with my fellow rural deans. There are fourteen rural deans, and apparently twelve responded. We were presumably all on much the same level of stipend. The published figures made interesting reading:

1 @ £34 per week, 1 @ £25 per week, 1 @ £15 per week, 2 @ £12.50 per week, 3 @ £11.50 per week, 1 @ £11 per week, 1 @ £10 per week, 1 @ £9 per week, and 1 @ £3 per week.

But the Diocese was unable to bring itself to quote those figures. Instead, in the Diocesan monthly news sheet, they saved any questioning, or embarrassment, or interest such figures might have had by publishing a composite figure: simply that the Rural Deans were giving – on average – £13.50 a week each! Was that a true reflection of the actual amounts given? It simply ignored the more sacrificial giving of some, which might have challenged the others, and perhaps spared the blushes of others. To my knowledge the Diocese did not publish the amounts being given by anyone else in the hierarchy. Interesting! I wonder why not?

Be that as it may, imagine the uproar if we were to propose a public receptacle in a prominent position in church for members' gifts to God? Perhaps a place where people could gather round to observe and publicly comment? No one can deny that such a practice would appear to have Scriptural warrant because Jesus Himself *sat, looked on and commented on people's giving*.[21] But to protect our right to privacy, some would say, 'When thou doest alms, let not thy left hand know what thy right hand doeth'.[22]

But that Scriptural reference has to do with 'alms', and not with the giving of tithes. The Good News Bible translation draws that out: 'When you help a *needy person* [this is what 'alms' or 'freewill offerings' are for], do it in such a way that even your closest friend will not know about it'.[23] It's an injunction given by Jesus to stop individuals bragging about their generosity to others. However, accountability for tithes is something else.

One can only question whether those who most vociferously speak out about the need for secrecy are ashamed to reveal what they give? As both a church and diocesan treasurer over many years, I know how the well-heeled often gave much less, proportionately, than the poorer members. You have probably heard of the wealthy member who threatened to withdraw his monthly pledge because he objected to policies approved by the PCC. The churchwarden told him not to worry on that score, because he personally wouldn't find it any hardship to add this man's '£1 a week' to his own pledge!

Sad to say 'shepherds' are often poor givers. Is it perhaps surprising many are in debt or suffer financial hardship? Some infer they give most, if not all, of their giving elsewhere. They need to start putting their money where their mouths are – the tithe to their local church, their freewill offerings elsewhere.

Show me a minister who believes in tithing, teaches the Biblical principle of tithing, and openly tithes to his local church as a matter of principle, and I will show you a church where the level of giving is well above average. No parson or lay leader can speak or preach effectively about giving, or have the right to ask or expect people to give generously and sacrificially, unless they are seen to lead by public example. And how dishonouring to God to find stewardship directors – and indeed their bishops – who neither tithe themselves, nor believe in the Biblical principle of tithing. Most people in God's House are taught man-made doctrines on principles of giving, rather than those given to us by God.

The Church (and I am thinking specifically of the Church of England here) has not always been so shy about the need for accountability. In the Church of England Prayer Book, produced in the sixteenth and seventeenth centuries, very clear guidelines were issued about giving.

'Yearly at Easter every parishioner shall reckon with the parson, vicar or curate, or his or their deputies; and pay to them or him all ecclesiastical duties accustomably due then and at that time to be paid.'[24] That was the tithe!

But note this also. All other giving during the year, through the collection plate, is clearly designated (in that same Prayer Book) as '*Alms for the poor*'; and *not*, equally clearly, *for the needs of the church*!

It was the Easter tithe, declared and paid to the vicar, that had to cover the expenses of maintaining the ongoing work, ministry and fabric of the church. It was clearly in line with God's injunction in Malachi to 'bring your tithes into the storehouse of the Temple'.

Equally clear by definition, the Sunday by Sunday offerings are what Scripture refers to as the people's 'Freewill Offerings' or *alms*. The use of these offerings were clearly set aside for charitable purposes only – i.e. to meet the needs of the poor and distressed.

To summarise:

THE TITHE was *openly declared* to the minister, or those appointed to represent him, and paid to him or them.

THE FREEWILL OFFERINGS, on the other hand, *remain secret* and are for the poor and needy.

The Church needs to return to such Biblical principles. If it did, not only local, but also regional and national church funding problems would end. There would be plenty and to spare not only to meet present expenditure on manpower and buildings, but also the requirements needed for re-evangelizing the nation. What a turn-around that would be for the Church!

NOTES:

1. Mal. 3:10
2. *Rain in a Dry Land* (Hodder and Stoughton 1986) – See 'Power of God in Giving' (Personal) pp. 157–165; and 'Power of God in Giving' (Church) pp. 166–176
3. 2 Cor. 9:7 (*RSV*)
4. Gen. 14:17–20
5. Mal. 3:10
6. 1 Cor. 16:1–4 – the word Paul uses for what they were doing to help the poor in Jerusalem was 'an extra collection', an 'extra piece of giving'; one that inferred it was over and above the normal collection or tithes of members to their local church.
7. Matt. 23:23
8. Matt. 10:16b (*KJV*)
9. Heb. 10:23; see also Heb. 11:11
10. 1 Kings 17:1–15
11. Matt. 19:16–22
12. Matt. 19:24
13. Luke 9:55 (*KJV*)
14. Matt. 16:23 (*KJV*)
15. Mark 12:41ff; Luke 21:1–4
16. Matt. 15:14
17. Matt. 23:16
18. Matt. 23:13
19. Mal. 3:10
20. Matt. 22:17–21b
21. Luke 21:1–4; Mark 12:41–44
22. Matt. 6:3 (*KJV*)
23. ibid., see note 15
24. Rubric in 1662 Prayer Book

Chapter 13

WHO IS THIS JESUS?

One of the extraordinary features of living today is the intrusiveness of the media. Heaven preserve any who become the focal point of their attention. No part of a person's life is above investigation – by fair, foul or deliberately smeared means. Like a pack of hounds, journalists and cameramen will besiege the home of the latest person they have judged fair game, with the besieged person feeling like the quarry run to earth. There, and at every other place the person is thought to frequent, the pack sit encamped, day and night, with their all-seeing and probing cameras, making those they target virtual prisoners.

No laws of the land appear sacrosanct here. Those victimised are branded as guilty – sometimes without any proven evidence. Unlike the procedure of the courts, the onus is on 'the persecuted' to prove their innocence. When they sally out, they run the ignominious gauntlet of those who not only barge, push, taunt, and probe but threaten them with a vast array of cameras, microphones and recorders. Is it any different from running the gauntlet of punishment? The hounding of Princess Diana still haunts us.

This, in some sections of our community, is today's abrasive investigative journalism. All too often their actions are accompanied without assurance that things said or done will be fairly reported, or reported unedited and unabridged.

Media 'trials' can pre-empt fair trials. They preclude 'you-are-innocent-until-proved-guilty' procedures. All too often we witness media trials presided over by pharisaical media editors and TV personalities assuming the role of judge and jury.

Pity those falsely accused. For most there is no redress because they cannot afford the cost of pursuing a libel action. The only recourse for some is a move to a secret address because of the 'crime' they were presumed to have committed.

What of those who are not permitted to grieve in private? It wasn't very different in the time of Jesus! Here the scrutiny of the media was replaced by arrogant, self-righteous chief priests, scribes, and pharisees. Heaven help you (literally) if they latched on to you, and got you in their clutches! Illegal trials in the middle of the night, with uncorroborated evidence and intimidation of witnesses, were likely. Jesus died as the result of one such 'trial'.

Equally true, there were times when the standard of their investigative journalism was pretty shoddy. They were not above publishing false 'facts' which resulted in the deliberate drawing of false conclusions. The conclusions reached about Jesus resulted in them misunderstanding and misrepresenting the greatest event in history.

Listen to this incident:

> Some of the people . . . said, 'This man is really the Prophet!' Others said, 'He is the Messiah!' But others said, 'The Messiah will not come from Galilee! The scripture says that the Messiah will be a descendant of King David and will be born in Bethlehem.'[1]
>
> . . . Some wanted to seize Him, but no one laid a hand on Him. When the guards went back, the chief priests and Pharisees asked them, 'Why did you not bring Him?' The guards answered, 'Nobody has ever talked liked this man!' 'Did He fool you, too?' the Pharisees asked. 'Have you ever known one of the authorities or one Pharisee to believe in Him? This crowd does not know the Law of Moses, so they are under God's curse!'
>
> One of the Pharisees there was Nicodemus, the man who had gone to see Jesus before[2]. He said to the others, 'According to our

Who Is This Jesus?

Law we cannot condemn a man before hearing him and finding out what he has done.' 'Well', they answered, 'are you also from Galilee? Study the Scriptures and you will learn that no prophet ever comes from Galilee.'[3]

They had checked back far enough to know he was from Nazareth in Galilee. How often, I wonder, did Jesus and others try to correct that information about his birthplace? And is it just possible they *were* given the information, but refused to accept it because it seriously undermined a major factor in their denial of his Messiahship? It wouldn't have been the only time they were challenged. Jesus specifically challenged them about His rightful claim to be the Messiah. There were many occasions in Jesus' ministry when the leaders were present – listening to Him teaching, observing His ministry, questioning Him, challenging Him.[4]

What might not be so well known is that there is a pattern that explains it. When we look at the Scriptures, sometimes the scribes and Pharisees are reported as observing Jesus silently, questioning Him only in their minds. At other times they are reported as being deliberately provocative; challenging Him and questioning Him openly; sometimes trying to trap Him with barbed or loaded questions.

So what is this pattern? About a hundred years before Christ was born, when false Messiahs were appearing, some of the rabbinical schools undertook an appraisal of their ministry. Their attention was drawn to two significant areas of healing and deliverance where no results had been noted.

One was the healing of lepers, which they believed had not taken place since the time of the Mosaic Law. The other was in casting out of evil spirits from a deaf and dumb person. It *was* possible to cast out evil spirits from those who *could* hear and speak, because the name(s) of the spirit(s) could be identified by asking the possessed person. But a deaf and dumb person could neither hear the question, nor answer it.

They concluded that only a true Messiah would be able to heal lepers or deal with evil spirits in the deaf and dumb category. So if these particular categories of miracles *were* performed, then there would be good reason to surmise that the performer might well be the Messiah.

If a leper was healed, then the procedures outlined in Leviticus, for the healing of lepers, were to be fully observed:
i) the healed leper must immediately present himself to a priest;
ii) he would be required to make all the various offerings outlined in Leviticus; these to include the trespass offering, the sin offering, the burnt offering, and the meal offering, together with the blood rituals and the anointing with oil.

But a very important part of the procedure would require the priest to assure himself:
i) the person really had been a leper;
ii) he had genuinely been healed of leprosy, and
iii) he considered it to be a significant miracle.

If the priest satisfied himself on all counts, the next step was to identify the person who had performed the healing and:
i) check out this person's ministry; and
ii) establish whether or not it was significant enough for him to be the possible Messiah.

There were two stages in this observation:

i) The Observation Stage. Jewish leaders from every part of Israel – Jerusalem, Judaea and Galilee – would be summoned as quickly as possible, and required to observe this person at work. During this observation period they were not allowed to discuss anything with, make comments to, or ask questions of the 'healer' for a period of seven days. They were to sit in silent judgement on his way of life, his teachings, his ministry, and note any miracles that might take place.

If at the end of that period the representative leaders from throughout Israel agreed together amongst themselves that this ministry appeared to have some significance, then they would proceed with the second stage:

ii) The Interrogation Stage. From now on there would be no holds barred.

Who Is This Jesus?

They were required to check out, question, and cross examine everything about the man: his way of life, his teachings, and any miracle or healing or deliverance performed by him.

Jewish leaders believed that by following these procedures, they would soon sort out the men from the boys, and enable them to deal with the charlatans. In the very early days of Jesus' ministry, Luke reveals amazingly clear indications of this procedure at work. They are to be found in all the Gospels, once one knows what one is looking for.

One of Jesus' earliest miracles was the healing of a leper. With hindsight, I don't believe this was fortuitous. Jesus used this opportunity to declare Himself for who He really was. Then He told the healed leper to go and show himself to the priest.

> The man 'threw himself down and begged Him, "Sir, if you want to, You can make me clean!" Jesus stretched out His hand and touched him. "I do want to," He answered. "Be clean!" At once the disease left the man. Jesus ordered him, "Don't tell anyone, but go straight to the priest and let him examine you; then to prove to everyone that you are cured, offer the sacrifice as Moses ordered."'[6]

Not surprisingly, considering the scale of the miracle, we are told after this that 'crowds of people came to hear Him and were healed from their diseases'.[7]

But then take careful note of what follows. Reading between the lines, so to speak, the priest who had seen the healed leper had obviously decided this was indeed one of those 'significant miracles'. Further, one can see that as soon as he could, he had instituted the first part of the investigative procedure:

Stage One: The Observation.
'One day when Jesus was teaching, some Pharisees and teachers of the Law were sitting there who had come from *every* town *in Galilee, Judaea and from Jerusalem*'.[8] Now that was no mean exercise to gather

together Jewish leaders from every town in all those areas. Imagine it religious leaders representative of at least every significant synagogue as well as the Temple, from every part of Israel!

But also notice the way they behave and react. Luke tells us 'the power of the Lord was present for Jesus to heal the sick'.[9] These leaders were not going to be disappointed after all the hype in getting them there to observe this 'healer'. Then follows the wonderful story of the paralysed man being let down through the roof of the house.

It is important to remember that the purpose of the religious leaders presence there was not only to establish whether this 'healer' had a significant ministry, but also, because *a leper* had been healed, to assess whether there was any possibility that this might be the Messiah. And Jesus, if we follow this theory, decides to openly follow up His claim to be the Messiah (on healing the leper) by declaring that claim afresh. So He says to the lame man: 'Your sins are forgiven, my friend.'[10]

He could not have said anything more likely to enrage the religious leaders. Their understanding of theology correctly stated that only GOD could forgive sins. But, because they are still in the Observation Stage, they are *not* allowed to say anything to Him *or* question Him. That is why Luke records this fact: 'the teachers of the Law and the Pharisees (remember they were all seated so they could carefully observe everything that went on) began to say *to themselves* (i.e. muttering under their breath) "Who is this man who speaks such blasphemy? God is the only one who can forgive sins!"'[11] Jesus has got them exactly where he wanted them with regard to His claim to be the Messiah. So, as modern parlance would have it, He went for the jugular!

> Jesus knew their thoughts and said to them, 'Why do you think such things? Is it easier to say, "Your sins are forgiven you", or to say, "Get up and walk"? I will prove to you, then, that the Son of Man has authority on earth to forgive sins." So He said to the paralysed man, "I tell you, get up, pick up your bed, and go home!" At once the man got up in front of them all, took the bed he had been lying on, and went home, praising God. They were all

completely amazed!'[12]

Of course it would have been much easier to say 'Your sins are forgiven' – because there is absolutely no way of proving whether a person's sins have been forgiven or not. So Jesus 'puts His money where His mouth is' and does something probably no one else would have dared to do in such circumstances. Especially when one considers all those religious leaders sitting in judgement on the effectiveness or otherwise of His ministry!

Jesus also performed a deliverance of evil spirits from someone who virtually fitted the category of someone who was deaf and dumb – this one being blind and dumb. In this incident also, the priests were still in the Observation Stage. We know that to be so, because after the evil spirit was driven out, the crowds were amazed and asked if Jesus could be the Son of David – the Messiah: 'they replied [obviously to themselves – or in asides to those round them] "He drives out demons only because their ruler Beelzebul gives him power to do so." Jesus *knew what they were thinking* . . .'[13] And so He challenges them; just as you drive out evil spirits by the power of God, so do I! But of course the significance of it all was that the dumb man had been unable to 'name' the spirit to be delivered. Jesus was able to do so by *discerning* the spirit.

Stage Two: The Interrogation.
In looking through the Gospels it is quite easy to note when they were into the Interrogation stage! For much of His ministry the crowds marvelled and were amazed at all they saw and heard. But for the teachers of the Law, the chief priests, the scribes, and the Pharisees, it was one long period of interrogation and confrontation. But despite all the evidence, including healing a leper and driving out evil spirits from someone who was blind and dumb, the leaders of Israel refused to acknowledge Jesus as their Messiah. So what more could He possibly do to convince them? In the range and breadth and sheer number of miracles, there had never been anyone like Jesus. But acknowledge

Him for who He really was, they would not!

It is in the light of this fact that we need to read the story of the Ten Lepers. It is almost as if Jesus says: you refuse to acknowledge Me when I heal a leper; you refuse to acknowledge Me when I drive out an evil spirit from someone who was dumb; what will your response be when I heal *ten* lepers? This time, much later on in His ministry, He was on His way to Jerusalem when He met the ten lepers outside a village between Samaria and Galilee: 'They stood at a distance and shouted, "Jesus! Master! Take pity on us"! Jesus saw them and said to them, "Go and let the priests examine you". On the way they were made clean.'[14]

What, we wonder, would the priests make of that incredibly significant miracle – not just *one* leper healed, but *ten*? With hindsight we know the answer to that. It appears then that from the very start of His ministry Jesus openly declared who He was. But the religious leaders would have none of it. Why? Because Jesus lacked the right qualifications? Or was it because He had not undergone the required 'theological' training? Or was it simply because He was not one of them – a priest, scribe, Pharisee or Sadducee? One recognises the professional jealousy. It is something which is no less prevalent in the hierarchical structures of the churches today!

Or was it because Jesus challenged the teachings of the religious leaders? Their Pharisaic and Mishnaic laws, and their traditions had become more important to them than the laws God had given through Moses:

'It is no use for them to worship Me, because they teach human rules as though they were My laws!'[15] 'How terrible for you, teachers of the Law and Pharisees! You hypocrites! You lock the door to the Kingdom of Heaven in people's faces, and you yourselves don't go in, nor do you allow in those who are trying to enter!'[16]

This surely must make us question the way we categorize what is a valid ministry or sacrament, or what makes one eligible for any given ministry. On what laws or requirements, different as they are for every denomination, do we assess what makes a valid ministry or sacrament?

Will it be only those who have fulfilled all their own denominational requirements? If those are the only legitimate ones (in our eyes), then what of the ministries and sacraments of other denominations? Are they of God, or are they not?

Like the 'religious law makers' or 'tradition-setters' of Jesus' day, we refuse to truly acknowledge the ministries of many because they don't fit our denominational strictures for performing valid sacraments or ministries. Surely the more important criteria should be: do we see the touch of God upon their lives and ministries? Do we see them bearing fruit for the kingdom of God? The one important question many refuse to face, as the law-givers did with Jesus, is this: does this person's ministry exhibit signs of God's anointing upon it?

In the time of Jesus, Pharisees and Sadducees and all manner of rabbinical schools defended their little empires for all they were worth, without noting, as Jesus so clearly demonstrated, what God was doing. So it is today! There has to be more than a suspicion that each denomination is behaving in exactly the same way: defending their own kingdom building, their own requirements and regulations for all they are worth. Much of it to do with wielding power, and who controls it. That is why it is so difficult for denominations to accept one another's ministries, or for ecumenical projects to succeed. In two thousand years we have learnt little. We are in danger of heading further and further down the same road . . .

Nothing will change until the Church does a complete about turn and begins to seek *God's* agenda, and *only* His agenda. There is a vital urgency to re-evaluate all we do (as individuals, congregations, and denominations) in terms of that agenda. Ultimately, man-made or man-centred kingdoms will crumble and come to nothing. God will simply move on and use those who are attuned to what HE is doing, and are concerned with what HE requires.

NOTES:
[1] See prophecies concerning this in 2 Sam. 7:12; Micah 5:2
[2] See John 3:1–2
[3] John 7:40:52

4. Messianic Jews are those Jews who have come to accept Jesus as their Messiah and Lord and Saviour. They help us see the Jewish New Testament scriptures from a Jewish perspective, and bring us wonderful insights and understanding. I have been richly blessed by a number of these Jewish scholars, particularly Arnold Fruchtenbaum. In this context I have been particularly helped by him to understand what he refers to as the *Observation and Interrogation* stages of Jesus' ministry. Books, audio and video cassettes of some of these authors can be had from: Anchor Recordings Ltd., 72, The Street, Kennington, Ashford, Kent TN24 9HS UK.
5. See 2 Kings 5 : Naaman, the commander of the Syrian army, had a dreaded skin disease (sometimes described erroneously as leprosy – but his whole army would have been decimated if he had been leprous; no nation would have risked that!)
6. Luke 5:12–14 (See also Matt. 8:2; Mark 1:40)
7. See Luke 5:15
8. Luke 5:17
9. Luke 5:17b
10. Luke 5:20b
11. Luke 5:21
12. Luke 5:22–26a
13. Matt. 12:24–25a
14. Luke 17:11–14
15. Matt. 15:9
16. Matt. 23:13

Chapter 14

THE PARABLE OF THE EAGLE

Some people describe the book of Isaiah as a Bible-in-miniature. Isaiah has 66 chapters; the Bible has 66 books! Further, some scholars suggest Isaiah was written by two people at quite different times (some even suggest three). They call the dual authors Isaiah, and Deutero-Isaiah. Following this theory, they suggest Isaiah wrote the first thirty-nine chapters, while 'second' Isaiah wrote the last twenty-seven chapters. 39 and 27. So, continuing with our analogy of Isaiah as a Bible-in-miniature: First Isaiah has 39 chapters, and the Old Testament 39 books. Second Isaiah has 27 chapters, and the New Testament 27 books!

One reason why some scholars find the idea of a single 'Isaiah' difficult is this. The author of the first thirty-nine chapters could not have known many of the facts of future history revealed in chapters 40 to 66. I would not presume to enter that argument, except to ask if they are looking at the evidence more from the standpoint of human reason, than giving weight to such spiritual gifts as knowledge and prophecy that many prophets clearly exercised?

The foretelling of future events, and here we must take into account all the notable prophecies concerning the future Messiah, is what much of our faith is built on. And it is extraordinary, isn't it, how much detail we are given concerning Jesus' forthcoming birth, life, death and Resurrection – much of it revealed to prophets with just such a gift many hundreds of years in advance of His birth! From that standpoint, I have no reason to doubt – despite what I was taught at Theological

College – that Isaiah was the author of the whole book. But each person has to make up his or her own mind on the basis of the evidence.

To state the obvious, the Old Testament deals with pre-Christian history, and the New Testament with the history of Christ and His first century Church.

Very generally speaking the first thirty-nine chapters of Isaiah speak of Israel's seesaw relationship with God over a long period of time. In this section Isaiah records how often God's people failed Him in that relationship, and underlines their recurring disobedience, and their frequent turning away to follow other gods.

The second part of Isaiah on the other hand – and again very generally speaking – speaks much of future change, but especially of the Messiah's role in that future. Who can fail to be amazed at the graphic details, and predictions, concerning Messiah's death in paying the penalty for man's sin?[1] It was given in all this detail over 700 *years* before He came to earth!

If we accept this division of the old and the new for the book of Isaiah, then we would expect to find a quite different emphasis in the key chapter – chapter forty. And there is! We'll return to that in a moment.

The problem for Isaiah is this. In those first thirty-nine chapters he has reported on the evidence of man's recurring failure for centuries past. This is a fact of history. The failures of God's people in their relationship with God, despite God's many interventions in wonderful and miraculous ways, is beyond comprehension! So the question Isaiah finds himself considering is this: was there any hope of improvement in the future, even if the Messiah came? Was there anything God could do that would make this new and restored relationship more likely to succeed?

And the glory of chapter forty is this. Isaiah triumphantly declares that it will be *significantly* different! It will be different because God will deal not only with man's sin, but also with man's powerlessness.

We return to the analogy of Isaiah's Bible-in-miniature. Chapter forty should reflect the beginnings of the New Testament. And it does –

The Parable of the Eagle

powerfully, dramatically, and in close detail considering it was prophesied 700 years before the events took place!

The chapter starts with God's promise of a glorious restoration: '"Comfort my people," says our God. "Comfort them! Encourage the people of Jerusalem. Tell them they have suffered long enough and their sins are now forgiven. I have punished them in full for all their sins."'[2]

The restoration is heralded by a lone voice in the wilderness: 'A voice cries out, "Prepare in the wilderness a road for the Lord! Clear the way in the desert for our God! Fill every valley; level every mountain. The hills will become a plain, and the rough country will be made smooth."'[3] We recognise 'the voice' as that of John the Baptist,[4] Jesus' cousin, announcing the coming of the Messiah Himself: 'Then the glory of the Lord will be revealed, and all mankind will see it. The Lord Himself has promised this'.[5]

It is such good news, it will be proclaimed everywhere. 'The Sovereign Lord is coming to rule with power, bringing with him the people he has rescued. He will take care of his flock like a shepherd; He will gather the lambs together and carry them in His arms; He will gently lead their mothers'.[6] The shepherd role of the Messiah (Jesus said, 'I am the Good Shepherd') is clear.

Isaiah is so overcome by God's continuing acts of forgiveness, and the promise of a yet more wonderful intervention in history by the Messiah Himself, that he bursts into a hymn of praise about this awesome God.

But deep within, Isaiah is still questioning. On the one hand, the just and holy, loving, endlessly compassionate, and yet ever forgiving God; on the other, sinful man who, however hard he tries, still frequently fails this all-holy God!

So God responds to Isaiah's questioning with a promise:

Israel, why then do you complain that the Lord doesn't know your troubles or care if you suffer injustice? Don't you know? Haven't you heard? The Lord is the everlasting God; He created

To Reign or Not to Reign

all the world. He never grows tired or weary. No one understands His thoughts.[7]

And that, in a sense, hits home at the nub of Isaiah's questioning – what hope is there if even young, healthy and active people find themselves getting tired and exhausted? God's answer?

He strengthens those who are weak and tired. Even those who are young grow weak; young people can fall exhausted. But those who trust in the Lord for help will find their strength renewed. They will rise on wings like eagles; they will run and not get weary; they will walk and not grow weak.[8]

The answer is in the last sentence of this fortieth chapter: the parable of the eagle. The significance of this parable is 'they will run and not get weary; they will walk and not grow weak'.[9] Those words would hold deep significance for Isaiah. They reminded him of an event in history that was as recent as are the high points in Queen Victoria's reign to us, and as well known . . .

They would have taken him back to Elijah's dramatic confrontation with the prophets of Baal on Mount Carmel. For three years they had suffered a terrible drought. Elijah revealed Baal's total ineffectiveness in the way he disposed of those false prophets, and revealed the power of the living God to a fickle people. With the return, as a result, of the people to the true and living God, Elijah believed it right to call on God to end the drought.

After much interceding by Elijah with God – and frequent trips by his servant to see if he can see anything – the latter finally returns with the news: 'I saw a little cloud no bigger than a man's hand, coming from the sea'.[10] So Elijah orders the servant to tell King Ahab to get back to Jezreel before the storm breaks. The King did as he was asked, mounted his chariot, 'and started back to Jezreel'.[11] We need to take note of the fact that being a king, Ahab without doubt would have had the finest horses money could procure.

The Parable of the Eagle

So note what follows: 'The *power* of the Lord came on Elijah; he fastened his clothes tight round his waist *and ran ahead of Ahab all the way to Jezreel*'![12] Elijah, for a glorious moment in time, was clothed with God's supernatural power!

A hundred years after Isaiah's time, and 200 years after the event at Mount Carmel, yet another prophet is reminded of that particular miracle. Jeremiah often felt inadequate for the task God had given him. And on one of those occasions God had to say to him: 'Jeremiah, if you get tired racing against people, how can you race against horses'![13] So like Isaiah, Jeremiah too would have found God's words – 'they will run and not get weary; they will walk and not grow weak' – deeply significant.

So what is the significance of the parable of the eagle? In many countries eagles nest at the top of very high cliffs. Because of the strength of the winds in such vulnerable places, the nests have to be both strong and securely fixed. So they are often woven with thorn branches and padded with feathers and other materials to make a soft bed for the family. After the little ones are hatched, they have a marvellous life. They eat and sleep and daydream. And the view is stupendous!

But when the time comes for them to get out and about, the mother eagle tears all the lining out of the nest. This leaves a very uncomfortable nest to be in. The eaglets begin to question parental affection!

Then suddenly and without warning, mother unceremoniously kicks a little one out of the nest and over the edge. As it gathers momentum down the cliff face, one can imagine the conversation it has with itself . . . 'I thought Mum loved me . . . I think this is the end . . . All that will be left of me will be a bloody mess on the rocks at the base of this cliff!' But, just before that happens, Mum swoops underneath and catches the little one on her back . . . 'Whew!' the eaglet murmurs . . . as Mum flies back to the cliff top and deposits the little one back in the nest! 'Just for a moment I thought you didn't care,' the little one is thinking, with its heart going like the clappers in its tiny little breast.

But without further ceremony Mum administers another kick to the posterior and it's over the edge we go again! Depending on how quick the little one is at learning, it might take several similar trips down the cliff face before the germ of an idea is planted in its brain. 'Perhaps if I flap my wings like Mum and Dad do?' . . . and the miracle happens. It doesn't fly far, but it is able to get to a rock ledge and finally makes its own way back up to the top.

And then there is the exhilarating sense of achievement and freedom that follows! Soon it is flying with considerable skill and power. But for an eagle, that is not the end of the learning process. All it has learnt to do so far is to fly in its own strength! Just as we learn to walk and run in our own strength.

And then one day, by carefully observing its parents, the eaglet learns that there is a way of flying that is way beyond anything it can do by flapping its wings in its own strength. And that is by discovering the thermals of God!

When a severe storm is brewing, the eagle learns to find an up-thermal, locks its wings in the outstretched position, and is carried at enormous speed way above the storm clouds. And when the storm is over, it descends at similar speeds in a down-thermal – all without having to flap its wings! It has learnt the ultimate technique – flying in the power of 'the wind that God supplies' rather than in its own strength.

That is the message God wants Isaiah to hear. That is the message for us to hear, and to understand. God's promise is simply this. After the coming of the Messiah, He will pour out His empowering spirit on all within His Church who want to receive it. No longer will people need to do things in their own strength. Supernatural gifts will be made available for those who seek them.

So Isaiah 40, that pivotal chapter, heralds the promise of a totally new era. It's to be ushered in by John the Baptist. Then comes the long awaited Messiah with the assurance of bringing about forgiveness and restoration. And finally the Messiah empowers all who are open to receive the outpouring of His Spirit for their work of ministry to a lost world!

However, that is not all that Isaiah 40 speaks about. There is one further issue. In giving a first hint of the Holy Spirit's work in God's

The Parable of the Eagle

new initiative, His people are warned of the consequences of lives and worship that are dishonouring to God, and of shepherds and religious leaders who hijack the faith.

> A voice cries out, 'Proclaim a message!' 'What message shall I proclaim?' I ask. 'Proclaim that all mankind are like grass; they last no longer than wild flowers. Grass withers and flowers fade, when the Lord sends the wind blowing over them. People are no more enduring than grass.'[14]

Something that happened over 700 years later helps us to understand the significance of this.

> When John saw many Pharisees and Sadducees coming to him to be baptized, he said to them, 'You snakes – who told you that you could escape from the punishment God is about to send? Do those things that will show that you have turned from your sins. And don't think you can escape punishment by saying that Abraham is your ancestor . . . the axe is ready to cut down the trees at the roots; every tree that does not bear good fruit will be cut down and thrown in the fire.'[15]

Jesus also had a great deal to say, and was not very complimentary at that, to the religious leaders of his day. He describes them as ravening wolves in sheep's clothing, as false shepherds, as whited sepulchres, as people who shut the doors to the Kingdom of heaven in people's faces.

Those warnings are for every age of the Church, particularly when it becomes powerless, moribund, and little better than a body of people worshipping pagan idols – whether it be a golden calf or a church building, or whatever. Isaiah 40 says something quite devastating about God's reaction to this state of affairs: 'Grass withers and flowers fade, when *the Lord sends the wind* blowing over them . . . Yes, grass withers and flowers fade, but the word of our God endures for ever.'[16]

To Reign or Not to Reign

We tend to think of the Holy Spirit as creative. In Genesis, the Holy Spirit brooded over the face of the waters[17] and brought order out of chaos. The Holy Spirit is also seen as a teacher, as the One who will lead us into all truth, and whose role it is to bring everything to our remembrance. We think of Him as giving new life; as tongues of fire; as the One who empowers.

But this passage in Isaiah speaks of the Holy Spirit as someone who breathes *death*! That is *not* something we usually consider. But yes! His role includes breathing death into everything that is not of God.

That has tremendous significance, and explains situations we find perplexing. For instance, many are rightly concerned when church congregations sometimes 'fall apart' when 'renewal' touches them. Some would even go so far as to say that this 'new thing' must be evil if it sows dissension and strife.

But there are facts that need to be faced, unpleasant though they may be. Some supposedly Christian congregations exhibit little more than what can only be described as folk or cult religion, or religiosity. Much of what they stand for is opposed to a Christ-centred faith.

For some, the observance of long held traditions or festivals are *the focus* of attention. For others it might be the style of worship, or music, or the church building itself that has become *the focus*. Without realising it, 'those things' have become the *raison d'etre* of church life – the gods they have come to worship – instead of submitting to the lordship of Christ. Inevitably, in such circumstances, a challenge to their entrenched positions signals war. But make no mistake. The Holy Spirit will breathe death into such congregations.

The passage in Isaiah clearly states that before God can do a significant work in people's lives, or in their churches, Christ has to have the pre-eminence. And if people are not prepared to acknowledge His sovereignty, then the dead wood *will* be removed, and unfruitful trees pruned or cut down. It is a painful, but often necessary, process before a congregation can move forward and experience new life and growth.

And Scripture is equally clear about the consequences when it is the

The Parable of the Eagle

church leaders themselves, 'the false shepherds', who are the stumbling block to faith and growth. Like the Pharisees and Sadducees of New Testament times, they stamp on any signs of renewal, and everything that challenges their perceptions and traditions.

In the three years of his ministry, Jesus tirelessly strove to correct the false teachings and religiosity of his day, targeting the church leaders of the day – the priests, Pharisees and Sadducees – who held the reins of control. But having made no impression on that false bastion of the faith, Jesus drew the line and rejected them in the final week of His life.

On Palm Sunday, Jesus moved in to 'cleanse the temple' saying: 'It is written in the Scriptures that God said, "My Temple will be called a house of prayer." But you are making it a hideout for thieves!'[18] His actions infuriated the 'church' leadership. It gave them yet another reason for wanting to put this troublemaker to death. That same night Jesus slept at Bethany (the Hebrew word means 'House of the Poor'). He always stayed with the poor – with those unable to afford to live within the security the city walls of Jerusalem provided.

Next morning, the Monday of Holy Week, He walked back over the Mount of Olives to Jerusalem. We are told: 'Jesus was hungry. He saw a fig tree by the side of the road and went to it, but found nothing on it except leaves. So He said to the tree, "You will never again bear fruit!" At once the fig tree dried up'.[19]

On Tuesday morning when they passed the tree, the disciples were amazed to find the tree withered from its roots up! Many feel that this quite unreasonable act of resentment and anger by Jesus, against a totally inoffensive tree, quite out of character. Why would Jesus curse an innocent tree for not having figs, when it wasn't even the season for figs?

Jesus had nothing against the tree! What he *was* doing was a symbolic act. The fig tree in Jewish life represented the nation.[20] And in clear and unmistakable terms, Jesus was proclaiming His judgement on the false religiosity of Israel, and on its religious leaders. He literally cursed them, and cut them off. He clearly fulfilled the requirement of Isaiah 40: 'Grass withers and flowers fade when the Lord sends the wind blowing over them'.[21]

And God breathes death into lifeless churches today. In cursing the fig tree, Jesus cleared the way for the establishment of a new 'Church' – for those who *would* believe, be obedient, and receive the empowering of the Holy Spirit after His Resurrection.

Jesus clarifies this a day or so later:

> Let the fig tree teach you a lesson. When its branches become green and tender and it starts putting out leaves, you know that summer is near. In the same way, when you see all these things, you will know that the time is near, ready to begin. Remember that all these things will happen before the people now living have all died. Heaven and earth will pass away, but My words will never pass away.[22]

Some believe this is the one prophetic utterance of Jesus where He simply got it wrong! The context in which this passage occurs is at the time when Jesus answered the disciples' questions about the end of all things. He described all manner of signs that will point to the coming of the end. But the sign of the fig tree, He tells them, is the most significant one.

And some people believe he got it wrong because He said: 'Remember that all these things will happen before the people *now living* have all died'.[23] It is patently obvious the world did not come to an end in the first century AD!

But to correctly understand the prophecy, it's important to realize prophecy usually has both a present and a future fulfilment. Jerusalem *was* utterly destroyed, 'without one stone being left upon another'[24] – and everyone dispersed around the nations of the world *within the lifetime* of those living then. It took place, in clear fulfilment of Jesus' prophecy, in AD 70. That is a fact of history. The nation of Israel, the 'fig tree', was to all intents and purposes destroyed from the root up, just as Jesus had cursed the fig tree on the Monday in Holy Week.

But there is also a *future* fulfilment to that prophecy, when all things

The Parable of the Eagle

will finally be accomplished. And the clue, Jesus tells us, lies in the parable of the fig tree. 'Let the fig tree teach you a lesson', Jesus says. It is now dead, withered from the roots up. But wait . . . 'When its branches become green and tender and it starts putting out leaves, you know that summer is near.'[25]

What Jesus prophesied was that the fig tree, the nation of Israel, will come to life again, and be reborn as a nation. This has to be something for the record books! After almost *two thousand years*, Israel *was* re-established as a nation within its original territorial boundaries! Nowhere else in history has this amazing feat been repeated.

And it is to *this* generation – that is, those who see the restoration of Israel – that all will not die before Christ comes in glory, and everything is accomplished!

When will that be? It can't be far off, although it is not clear when the countdown actually started – or will start. Is it from the date in 1918 when Lord Balfour's declaration allowed the Jews to return to their original homeland? Is it from the date when Israel was established by United Nations charter in 1947? That was a miracle in itself getting all the permanent members of the Security Council – Russia included – to agree. Is it from the end of the 1967 Six-Day War when Israel regained control of Jerusalem and the Golan Heights? Or . . . ?

We can't be absolutely sure. Jesus warns us not to try and determine the day and the hour – because we can't. He will come at a moment when the world least expects Him. And all through the last two thousand years many people have predicted dates for Christ's return . . . and got it wrong! The Jehovah's Witnesses have fixed a date many times since the middle of the last century – and got it wrong every time.

That is not surprising, since this long list of dates was for dates prior to the 'key' sign given by Jesus, the fig tree coming back to life – signalling the re-establishment of Israel.

In the early months of pregnancy – a situation comparable to the period of history we are now in with the final countdown already in operation – even the finest gynarcologist cannot predict the exact day and the hour of the child's birth! But from all the available signs, together

To Reign or Not to Reign

with all the available information he is able to gather from the mother, he can make a fairly accurate prediction as to the likely period when the baby can be expected – give or take a few days or weeks.

In the same way, Paul tells us, we are not to be like worldly people who are unaware of the signs: '... you, brothers, are not in the darkness, and the Day should not take you by surprise like a thief'.[26]

Is it any wonder then, knowing Christ's concern for the lost, that there has been an unprecedented outpouring of the Spirit of God in power upon people of evey denomination – as well as almost simultaneously in every part of the world – in recent years? And was it surprising, taking these factors into consideration, that so many denominations, in so many parts of the world, all targeted the last decade of the last century as a decade of evangelism?

And is it surprising to find such unprecedented growth in the Christian church in the Third World – where the world's poorest are to be found, and where there are fewer intellectual blockages to the acceptance of the power gifts of the Holy Spirit?

But at the same time we are not to dismiss it and imagine it won't happen in our lifetime. It will happen, Jesus foretold, before all the people who have seen the fig tree come to life have died.

Paul, too, gives us a graphic illustration of what this factor should mean to us, and how we are to handle it:

> There is no need to write to you, brothers, about the times and occasions when these things [surrounding Christ's second coming] will happen. For you yourselves know very well that the Day of the Lord will come as a thief comes at night. When people say, 'Everything is quiet and safe,' then suddenly destruction will hit them![27]

That, says Paul, is how it will seem *to the worldly* – those who are not in on the secret. But this will not be the case where Christians are concerned. Just as we are now aware of Israel's rebirth – as the final sign given by Jesus to signal the beginning of the end – so we are not to

The Parable of the Eagle

be blind to what is happening. As Paul puts it: 'It will come as suddenly as the pains that come upon a woman in labour, and people will not escape. But you, brothers, are not in the darkness, and the Day should *not* take you by surprise like a thief'.[28]

Surely, in these remarkable ways, the Spirit of God is revealing the urgency of our times.

Is it surprising that in the western industrialised nations – and for more than a century – the Church experienced an ever-increasing loss of membership and resources? All too many churches and denominations have become locked into a maintenance ministry, and yet continue to lose ground? Would a reason for this be that they continue to lose ground because of the level of unbelief, or the denial of the promises of Scripture, or the rejection of God's supernatural gifts through the empowering of the Holy Spirit?

Our media have judged the Church – because of its perceived failures in the last century – to be largely irrelevant within our society. I believe there is actually a cry of anger at the Church's impotence contained within that judgement.

With the increasing recognition of the almost total breakdown of morality, law and order – in all our European and North American countries – people see no organisation to which they can turn to rectify this decadent downward spiral. Deep down they are crying out for some authority to rectify this situation before it is too late. In so many situations it has become a case of 'men's hearts failing them for fear'.[29]

Both media and politicians are seen as powerless to prevent the ever-increasing drift towards mayhem and total anarchy – with whole sections of society seemingly out of control. Almost overnight there is an awareness of the need for some agency to come to the rescue and rebuild society by restoring family relationships, the need for a return to Biblical values of morality!

One senses this anger becoming more strident. Why? Because the Church – the obvious agency to turn to in such issues – is so ineffective it might as well not exist for all the good it could do. Meanwhile, the Church itself is too busy naval-gazing to be able to respond – worrying

To Reign or Not to Reign

about its survival, discussing internal issues *ad nauseam*.

It was not so with Jesus: 'the Son of Man came to seek and to save the lost.[30] His commission to those within the fold is to search for the lost – and to leave no stone unturned until every lost sheep is found and brought back – with great rejoicing and celebration.

The Church blames the mess on anyone but itself. But it is the Church that God will hold responsible for the breakdown of the fabric of society and for all that there is within our society that is contrary to God's will and purpose.

Ezekiel writes:

> The Lord spoke to me. 'Mortal man,' He said, 'denounce the rulers . . . [the] shepherds of Israel! You take care of yourselves, but never tend the sheep . . . You have not taken care of the weak ones, healed those that are sick, bandaged those that are hurt, brought back those that wandered off, or looked for those that were lost. Instead, you treated them cruelly. Because the sheep had no shepherd, they were scattered, and wild animals killed and ate them. So My sheep wandered over the high hills and the mountains . . . My shepherds did not try to find the sheep. They were taking care of themselves and not the sheep. So listen to Me, you shepherds. I, the Sovereign Lord, declare that I am your enemy. I will take My sheep away from you and never again let you be . . . shepherds . . .'[31]

In another hard hitting prophecy, Ezekiel clearly speaks into our situation today, just as much as he did for his own:

> The leaders . . . take all the money and property they can get, and by their murders leave many widows. The priests break My law and have no respect for what is holy. They make no distinction between what is holy and what is not. They do not teach the difference between clean and unclean things, and they ignore the Sabbath. As a result the people of Israel do not respect Me . . .

The Parable of the Eagle

> The prophets have hidden these sins like men covering a wall with whitewash. They see false visions and make false predictions. They claim to speak the word of the Sovereign Lord, but I, the Lord, have not spoken to them.
>
> The wealthy cheat and rob. They ill-treat the poor and take advantage of foreigners. I looked for someone who could build a wall, who could stand in the places where the walls have crumbled and defend the land when My anger is about to destroy it, but I could find no one . . .[32]

It is the Church – not the world – that God gives the responsibility for bringing about change:

> If My people, who are called by My name, will humble themselves and pray and seek My face and turn from their wicked ways, then will I hear from heaven and will forgive their sin and will heal their land.[33]

Just as God holds us responsible – so too does society! We might find that hard to swallow considering the rubbishing the Church receives from the 'worldly-wise', but it is none the less true.

The Church is seen as having failed to hold the high ground. Its standards, its morality as evidenced by its growing permissiveness, and its belief-system are seen to be as suspect as those of society. And its implied acceptance of much that is advocated by our permissive society is seen as repugnant, and rightly so. The Church has signally failed to teach and live out the Christian ethic.

What society cries out for is a Church that is patently 'on fire' for God, unequivocal in all it stands for, and demonstrably using "the mighty strength which Christ supplies'.[34]

NOTES:
[1] See Isaiah 52:13 – 53:12
[2] Isa. 40:1–2
[3] Isa. 40:3–4

[4] See Matt. 3:1–3; Mark 1:1–3; Luke 3:1–6; John 1:19–28
[5] Isa. 40:5
[6] Isa. 40:10–11
[7] Isa. 40:27–28
[8] Isa. 40:29–31
[9] ibid.
[10] 1 Kings 18:44
[11] 1 Kings 18:45b
[12] 1 Kings 18:46
[13] Jer. 12:5a
[14] Isa. 40:6–7
[15] Matt. 3:7ff
[16] Isa. 40:7–8
[17] See Gen. 1:2
[18] Matt. 21:13 (cf Isa. 56:7)
[19] Matt. 21:18–19
[20] See Jer. 8.13 (cf Jer. 24.1–10)
[21] Isa. 40:7
[22] Matt. 24:32–35 (cf Mark 13:28–31; Luke 21:29–33)
[23] Matt. 24:34
[24] See Luke 21:6
[25] Matt. 24:32 (See also Luke 21:29–31; Mark 13:28)
[26] 1 Thess. 5:4
[27] 1 Thess. 5:1–3a
[28] 1 Thess. 5:3b–4
[29] Luke 21:26
[30] Luke 19:10 (See also Luke 15:9, 24 etc.)
[31] Ezek. 34:2–10 (See also Ezek. 3:17–19)
[32] Ezek. 22:25–30
[33] 2 Chr. 7:14 (*RSV*)
[34] Col. 1:29

Chapter 15

NOT RETIRED – RE-FIRED!

After Rolf retired as Vicar of Coopersale, we visited him and his wife Elisabeth in their new home in Bath. He was busy helping out in the hospital – this being his real love and ministry gifting – as well as in several local parishes. I asked him, tongue in cheek, how he enjoyed being retired. 'Not retired – re-fired!' he responded with a great chuckle.

I could think of no better answer to give! When you love the Lord, and been so empowered with the Holy Spirit as these two have these many years past, retirement is the last thing you have in mind.

Almost daily Rolf and Elisabeth see evidence of God powerfully at work in people's lives; they have that very special privilege of seeing new souls brought into the Kingdom; they are witnesses to so much healing in Jesus' name. They know time is short, because Christ will soon come again, as promised. So Rolf is not hanging up his dog collar. He's re-fired, not retired.

Many have been puzzled about a passage in Scripture that appears to contradict events as we know them. '. . . [John the Baptist] called two [of his disciples] and sent them to the Lord to ask Him, "Are You the one John said was to come, or should we expect someone else"?'[1]

The problem is this. John already knew the answer! So the incident makes absolutely no sense at this juncture. Why did he ask Jesus if He was the promised Messiah when he had known that to be true from the time Jesus was baptized? On that earlier occasion John had heard the voice from Heaven confirming that very fact about Jesus: 'You are My

To Reign or Not to Reign

own dear Son, I am pleased with You'. Further, he had actually seen the Holy Spirit, in the form of a dove, descend on Jesus at His baptism![2]

What is more, on the day following Jesus' baptism, we are told: 'John [the Baptist] was standing there again with two of his disciples, when he saw Jesus walking by. "There is the Lamb of God", he said. The two disciples heard him say this and went with Jesus.'[3] It is very clear from these earlier passages that John the Baptist had already recognised Jesus, and affirmed Him, as the Messiah, 'The Lamb of God'.

A considerable period of time passes. Finally John is put in prison. Why on earth does he *then* send two men to ask if 'You are the one John said was going to come, or if we should expect someone else?'[4]

The only obvious answers that come to mind are that he had suffered amnesia, or that his imprisonment had brought on a bout of acute depression. But neither of those reasons make any sense when we note the way Jesus reacted to John's messengers.

Jesus doesn't answer them! He seems to ignore them. Nor does He respond angrily. If I had been in Jesus' shoes I would probably have responded with some sarcasm – 'Is John's memory so short? Doesn't he remember what happened when he baptized Me at Jordan?'

However, Jesus' actual reaction is significant in helping us to unravel what was going on. Note the way Jesus initially responds to the question: 'At that very time Jesus cured many people of their sicknesses, diseases and evil spirits, and gave sight to many blind people.'[5] Only *then* did He turn and give an answer to the two men.

> . . . Go back and tell John what you have seen and heard: the blind can see, the lame can walk, those who suffer from dreaded skin diseases are made clean, the deaf can hear, the dead are raised to life, and the Good News is preached to the poor.[6]

Wait for it! Jesus then ends his reply with a seeming throw-away comment: 'How happy are those who have no doubts about Me'![7]

On reflection, perhaps John the Baptist did not doubt the anointing

Jesus received at His baptism at the river Jordan. Instead, was it rather a concern that the anointing itself might be lost?

The Old Testament speaks of many people anointed with the Spirit of God who then – through sin, rejection, or deliberate disobedience – lose that anointing. One has only to think of people like Eli, Saul, who consulted a witch at Endor instead of turning to God, David – for a period, at least, after committing adultery and arranging a murder – together with a multitude of unfaithful prophets and priests.

John the Baptist, also anointed with the Spirit, recognises that he faces possible death in prison. Was he fearful that Jesus might have lost, or might lose, His anointing? He would be fearful – from a human standpoint – because who then would continue with the work God had entrusted to them?

That, I believe, might explain why Jesus does not give an immediate verbal response to the two men who questioned him. Instead, He turns away and ministers to people's needs, with many signs and wonders being performed right there in front of their eyes. Then He turns to the two men – who must have waited patiently for quite some while for all that to take place – and, in effect, says: 'Go and tell John there is no need for him to be worried; you have seen for yourselves that God's anointing is still present in My ministry.'

But there are two further significant features to this incident for us to note. The first is this. Jesus shows no irritation or anger at the anointing on His ministry being called into question. In fact, the reverse is true. The way He reacts leads one to believe He thought it perfectly proper for people to question whether the anointing was still there. And any tense feelings the challenge might have caused are, I believe, generously removed by Jesus' final quip: 'How happy are those who have no doubts about Me!'[8] One can imagine a twinkle in His eye as he said it.

The second significant feature that strikes home is this. If people were given the green light to question Jesus about God's continued anointing in His ministry, then don't people have the right to question the anointing (or lack of it) in *our* ministries?

Many raise defence mechanisms, or become angry, if their anointing in ministry is challenged. Others feel defensive because they find themselves in a 'catch twenty-two' situation – expending much of their ministry on things that are not within their gifting, or in chores that really have little to do with the great commission.

It is this feature of the incident – the right to challenge, and the response – which makes this one of the most challenging passages in Scripture, certainly for me. We can't escape the fact that Jesus promised to give His Spirit's empowering to those who asked for it. His promise was simply this: 'Whoever believes in Me will do what I do – yes he will do even greater things, because I am going to the Father . . .'[9] Can you or I ever be satisfied with *less* than that full anointing?

There is no place in the ministry for those who are going to play it safe – just in case God does not respond! God looks for those willing to take Him at His Word, who trust in His promises, and are excited at the prospect of being used in doing great exploits for Him! Of course it's not easy. Doubts arise all too easily every single time we venture out in faith. What is essential is that we refuse to be conditioned or controlled by doubt or unbelief.

I am naturally a sceptic at heart. Every new area of ministry I have entered has brought heart-searching, questioning and doubts. Most times there is no easy way through this minefield. It has always been so, even for the greatest of the prophets and saints.

It wasn't easy for Abraham when he agreed to God's request that he sacrifice his only son Isaac. Every step of that road – right to the moment when God stayed the knife in Abraham's uplifted arm – must have been traumatic and heartrending in the extreme. Only when he was obedient and faithful to the last was God's provision (the ram caught in the thicket) finally revealed.

One incident that concerned me is but one example of the questioning raised in my own ministry. It reveals God's humour! For many years I was sceptical of what is variously described as 'resting in the Spirit' (the best description to my mind), or 'overcome by the Spirit' or 'falling under the power of the Spirit', or 'slain in the Spirit'. It is a not uncommon phenomenon in charismatic and Pentecostal circles. When people 'went down', I used to watch very carefully, for sometimes it seemed as though the person ministering pushed the person being prayed for – gentle pressure on the forehead for example – and so 'encouraged' the subject to go over backwards.

And I had experiences of ministers, on more than one occasion, who pushed me fairly forcefully on the forehead, and who showed irritation because I refused to go down and join the serried ranks of those lying on the floor around me.

Then there are the 'catchers' standing behind which can lead, amongst those prayed for, to an understanding that they are expected to fall down. It is this sort of psychology that could be at work, could it not, when women stewards stand by with gold embroidered squares – to keep women respectable when they have fallen prostrate on the floor?

All to easy, isn't it, for these things to become fads, and for everyone expected to jump on the bandwagon? Was the Holy Spirit really at work in such cases? I soon decided I wasn't going to be part of it, and quietly used my authority to frown on the practice when I was ministering. But it is also true that I have been present on a number of occasions when someone has gone down like the proverbial ninepin – with no catcher standing by – and experiencing no hurt whatever. After a while the practice no longer bugged me. In fact I hadn't consciously thought about it for ages until . . .

I had been invited to talk to a Full Gospel Business Men's Fellowship in Banbury. As the event drew closer, I realised I had been over-committed. I nearly telephoned to cry off, but realised it wouldn't be fair for them to have to find another speaker at such short notice. I'd had nearly a dozen speaking and preaching engagements in not much more than a week. (When do we ever learn to say 'No', more often?) I arrived in Banbury exhausted.

When I met with the leaders they asked me to speak, and then lead the time of ministry that followed. I agreed to speak, but explained I was too tired to undertake the ministry, and asked the local members to do that. Later that evening, when the ministry time began, quite a number

To Reign or Not to Reign

of people asked for prayer. I felt the best contribution I could make was to stay in my chair and pray. Much later in the evening the Chairman gave a final call for prayer for those . . . and I didn't hear what he said. But so many stood for prayer that all the rest were on their feet praying with them. All seemed to be cared for except for one woman in my corner of the room; no one was praying with her, and I realised she had been standing there a little while! I really didn't want to get up, but felt I had to respond to her need.

So, somewhat reluctantly, I moved over to her, put my hands ever so gently on her shoulders . . . and down she went like a pin in a bowling alley. I tried to hold her, but she was gone. Still needing rest – and realising she was virtually out cold on the floor there – I sauntered back to my seat. I suppose I had been out of it less than thirty seconds. Only then did I see the funny side of it as I became aware of a number of people looking at me in that quizzical way that said: If the Lord uses you like that, why haven't you been up ministering to us for the last half hour?

What they didn't know was that it had never happened to me before. And in case anyone gets any ideas, it has not happened to me very often since! The Lord certainly honoured my need for rest! I thought I could still hear Him chuckling as I drove home to Northampton shortly after. And the woman I ministered to for a brief moment? Simply overjoyed at the way Jesus had ministered to her over quite a long period of time as she lay there. I had not even begun to pray for her specific need!

Anyone interested in a superbly informative book on this subject should read Francis MacNutt's *Overcome by the Spirit*.[10] Francis is not only able to speak from a wealth of present day experience of this phenomenon, but has also – with his Roman Catholic priestly training and background – researched its activity in the lives of many of the great saints throughout history. It brings light into so many fascinating incidents.

During our ten years in Northampton, Jill and I held more than twenty intensive courses on the practical experience of the supernatural gifts of the Spirit as described in 1 Corinthians 12, and verses 8–10. That series of courses brought together well over 500 people in a seven-week commitment, three to four hours each week (plus homework), in a deep and close-knit fellowship. They came from Northamptonshire and several neighbouring counties, and a wide range of denominations.

Of those who attended, and they included quite a number of priests and ministers, probably something like 80 per cent experienced what some see as the controversial speaking in tongues – particularly as a prayer language – for the first time.

Although many in our mainstream denominations will have nothing to do with this gift, no less a person than Michael Ramsey, former Archbishop of Canterbury, strongly endorsed the importance of the spiritual gifts, including glossolalia or speaking in tongues. Speaking of this particular gift, he says:

> It is clearly not a sign of spiritual excellence, but it would be unfair to conclude from St Paul's warnings about its small value in the assemblies that he would belittle its place in the Christian life as a liberation of a Christian into a joyful outburst of praise. Ramsey further stresses that 'while the Spirit uses this shape' [worship patterns, traditions and teachings of the church etc.] the Spirit also acts in unpredictable ways, exposing, teaching, illuminating, judging, renewing. The Spirit is still the unpredictable ruach [the 'now' word of God to this generation] . . .[11]

Paul sees the gift of tongues as wonderfully helpful to us:
If I pray in this way, my spirit prays indeed, but my mind has no part of it. What should I do then? I will pray with my spirit, but I will pray also with my mind; I will sing with my spirit, but I will sing also with my mind . . .[12]
To understand that better, he tells us:

> The Spirit also comes to help us, weak as we are. For we do not

know how we ought to pray, the Spirit Himself pleads with God for us in groans that words cannot express. And God, who sees into our hearts, knows what the thought of the Spirit is; because the Spirit pleads with God on behalf of His people and in accordance with His will.[13]

So it is not surprising that Paul calls on all God's people to: 'Pray at all times in the Spirit, with all prayer and supplication. To that end,' he says, 'keep alert with all perseverance . . .'[14]

The reminder about perseverance is important, because all too many – having received the gift – no longer work at it. If Paul regards it as such an important gift, we should too; and he gives a clue as to why his own ministry was so effective, and so productive: 'I thank God that I speak in strange tongues much more than any of you'[15] He was speaking here of the gift of tongues as a prayer language.

That private prayer language is a gift for our own personal use, for our prayer times, and is available to everyone. The public use of tongues, on the other hand – which requires an interpretation – is not a gift which everyone necessarily has. If we understand this distinction, then much which is spoken about the gift of tongues[16] – and the two facets of the same gift – becomes clearer. It is the private prayer tongue that Paul expects everyone to ask for, and use – a gift needed when we just don't know how to pray, or what to ask for.[16]

However, many find Paul's treatment (1 Corinthians 14:20–25) of one particular aspect of the gift of tongues confusing. In this section he appears to contradict himself. So it is important to unravel it. The best way of explaining what he is saying is to give two examples.

If an unbeliever were to walk into a church and find everyone speaking in tongues, he would simply imagine everyone had gone stark raving mad. (Most church goers would show the same reaction!) Hence Paul's insistence that tongues, when used in public worship should be followed by an interpretation.

But there is the odd occasion when it *can* work! Some years ago a clergyman's wife told me she sometimes found herself speaking the strangest of sounds – could it be a tongue? (She had never had any teaching in this area before!) We suggested she use it in our next session – a weekend renewal with people from many places. After she did so, a young girl visiting us from Israel, astonished the woman by telling her she was speaking in faultless Hebrew (*not* a language she had ever studied!), and the words God had spoken through Leonie had meant so much to this Jewish girl!

Another incident concerns a priest who had been filled with the Spirit, and spoke in tongues. He was one of several in a congregation where renewal had begun to take place. However a number of unhappy experiences followed, and the priest turned his back on all of it, and forbade the use of all supernatural gifts in his church. Concerning his own experience, he convinced himself he had made up the tongue he had spoken. All this caused much hurt and pain in the church. But the others, who had also been touched by the Spirit, gently tried to coax the vicar into moving forward with the gifts once more. Each time they tried, he became more and more angry.

Some few years later, on being approached yet again, he was furious. He decided to scotch this once and for all. So the next Sunday he preached about false spirits. To conclude his sermon, he said anyone could make up a language and proceeded to show them what he could do – as he thought – by his own efforts.

He was dumbfounded when a visitor at the back of the Church confessed his faith in Christ, and explained that the clergyman had spoken God's word to him in his own home language – in a Chinese dialect!

So Paul is *not* contradicting himself in this passage; he simply says that a tongue without an interpretation – as happened on the day of Pentecost – can be very effective. But don't look to it as being the norm.

The prayer tongue is also a most valuable, indeed often essential, asset in ministering to others. A group silently praying in tongues can be waiting for God to reveal supernatural knowledge to pinpoint what to pray, or how to pray, for a person. A group is important, because God often reveals different aspects to different people – so enabling a composite picture of the person's need, or root problem, to be revealed by the Spirit. From our own experience, over quite a long period of time, the prayer tongue often triggers other supernatural gifts into use – such as wisdom, knowledge, healing, prophetic utterance and the like.

Of course the question that confounds most of us is this? Why did God choose such an extraordinary – and, let's face it, controversial – gift for us to use? Especially one that so often results in almost instant rejection? 'I'm not going to be made a laughing stock using such a gift!' 'What's wrong with my own mother tongue . . . ?' and so on.

Remember the Tower of Babylon? Why it was called Babel? Let me remind you of the story.

At first, the people of the whole world had only one language...[18] Then they decided to defy God.[19] By this stage in their history they saw themselves as so powerful and clever they could build a tower to get to heaven. And the Lord noted . . . 'soon they will ... do anything they want! Let Us go down and mix up their language so that they will not understand one another.'[20] He didn't send thunder or lightning. He just incapacitated them – by touching the tongue!

Two thousand years later God brought about a restoration – *by again touching the tongue*:

"When the day of Pentecost came . . . they were all filled with the Holy Spirit and began to talk in other languages, as the Spirit enabled them to speak'.[21] The assembled crowds, gathered in Jerusalem from every nation in the then known world, were astonished and said 'all of us hear them speaking in our own languages about the great things that God has done!' Amazed and confused, they kept asking each other, "What does this mean?"'[22]

The part of the body we find almost impossible to control is the tongue. James gives us a graphic picture of the power of the tongue – little as it is: 'Just think how large a forest can be set on fire by a tiny flame! And the tongue is like a fire!'[23] Interesting, isn't it, that the *symbol* of the Holy Spirit is also fire!

'No one has ever been able to tame the tongue'.[24] If God is really going to reign in our hearts and lives, and be Lord of every part of us, then we need to be able to surrender the tongue to the Spirit's control. That is why the gift of tongues is a gift not to be ignored.

Michael Ramsey spoke of the need for Christians to 'be filled with the Spirit, addressing one another in psalms and hymns and spiritual songs.[25] He says: 'It is in this context that glossolalia, or speaking with tongues may be significant [because it helps us] to cross the threshold [of our defences] and attain a new freedom in our surrender to God.'[26]

One last point regarding this most controversial of all the Spirit's gifts. Too often I hear people say, 'Yes! I long for all of the spiritual gifts – as long as it doesn't include the gift of tongues!'

We are never in a position to dictate terms to God! He does not permit us to lay down conditions. Either He is God, or He isn't! We either open ourselves to receive God's gifts under His terms, or not be surprised if we find ourselves denied all of the seven supernatural gifts! Perhaps that is why this gift involves the tongue – the part of the body we find hardest to control, or surrender control over! So naturally God asks, 'Are you willing to surrender everything to Me, even your tongue?'

For those who have difficulty in surrendering the tongue, take courage from Michael Ramsey:

It is a costly thing to invoke the Spirit, for the glory of Calvary was the cost of the Spirit's mission and is the cost of the Spirit's renewal. It is in the shadow of the cross that in any age of history Christians pray: Come, thou holy paraclete.[27]

One last comment about the gift of tongues, or glossolalia, as a prayer language. Unlike the other gifts listed in 1 Corinthians 12, it is *the* one supernatural gift God gives to benefit and build up the user personally. As one's prayer life improves, so the spiritual life is strengthened. It is for this very reason Satan hates this particular gift so much, and works

To Reign or Not to Reign

hard to cause as much confusion as possible in this area – and deny people's need of it.

NOTES:
1. Luke 7:18b,19
2. Luke 3:21,22
3. John 1:35–37
4. See Note 1 above
5. Luke 7:21
6. Luke 21:22
7. Luke 7:23
8. Luke 7:23
9. John 14:12
10. *Overcome by the Spirit* Francis MacNutt, (Published by Eagle of IPS Ltd. 1991)
11. *Holy Spirit* Michael Ramsey (SPCK 1977)
12. 1 Cor. 14:14–15
13. Rom. 8:26,27
14. Eph. 6:18b (*RSV*)
15. 1 Cor. 14:18
16. See 1 Cor. 14
17. Gift of tongues as a private prayer language: e.g. Rom. 8:26,27; 1 Cor. 14:5,6a, 7–11,16–18,28
    Gift of tongues as a public gift: e.g. 1 Cor. 14:5b,6b,12–13, N.B.19 (if no interpretation, 27
18. Gen. 11:1
19. See Gen. 11:4
20. Gen. 11:6,7
21. Acts 2:1,4
22. Acts 2:11b,12
23. James 3:5
24. James 3:8
25. Eph. 5:19 (*RSV*)
26. *Holy Spirit* Michael Ramsey (SPCK 1977)
27. ibid.

Chapter 16

NEW WINE FROM OLD SKINS

I mentioned in an earlier chapter Paul's 'gold thread' in relation to God's empowering Holy Spirit. 'This power working in us', he assures the Christians in Ephesus, 'is the same as the mighty strength which He used when He raised Christ from death and seated Him at His right side in the heavenly world'.[1]

This is a revelation and experience the Church needs to rediscover if we are to see the kind of Christian revival many of us are praying for – especially in Britain and Europe where it is so desperately needed. Paul gives a clear indication of what he means by this empowering.

If we are to understand the concept, it is important to have the eye of faith to understand the unexpected sequence of statements Paul gives us to reflect on. Many fail to see their significance. What is unfolded for us is this.

The people to whom he addresses his Ephesian letter are people He clearly acknowledges to be Christians who have received the gift of the Holy Spirit: 'You also became God's people when you heard the true message, the Good News that brought you salvation. You believed in Christ, and God put His stamp of ownership on you *by giving you the Holy Spirit* He had promised'.[2] 'For this reason, ever since I heard of your faith ... I have not stopped giving thanks . . .'[3]

But then note what follows: 'I remember you [i.e. the believers filled with the Spirit] in my prayers and ask the God of our Lord Jesus Christ, the glorious Father, to give you the Spirit . . .'

Now that doesn't seem to make sense. They already have the Holy Spirit. Paul acknowledged that. But to clarify this to his readers he goes on and says that he asks God: 'to give you the Spirit, who will make you wise and reveal God to you . . . and . . . [help you to] know how very great is His power at work in us who believe. *This power working in us is the same as* the mighty strength which He used when He raised Christ from death . . .'[5]

How could Paul pray for these people to be filled with the Holy Spirit as if they had never experienced it? Was he denying what he had said earlier in describing their standing in the Church – particularly in relation to the Holy Spirit? I don't believe so.

Although it is not so apparent in English translations, the Holy Spirit is referred to in the New Testament in either one of two clearly distinct ways. At first sight, and certainly in many modern languages, the distinction might seem laughable. But the distinction (and clearly in the original Greek it *is* significant) is that it is referred to as either '*the* Holy Spirit', or simply as 'Holy Spirit'.

When it talks about '*the* Holy Spirit' (and the word 'the' is used in the Greek), it always refers to the *person* of the Holy Spirit present within us – as our teacher, who leads us into all truth, and who brings God's truths to mind.

When 'Holy Spirit' (without the definite article 'the') is used, it always refers to the *Spirit's power being released*, or manifested, in us or through us. (I have already written on this in some detail in *Rain in a Dry Land*, but a brief summary of the references are given in the accompanying note if you want to check them out for yourself.)[6]

But it speaks of something that is very important for all to understand. One can receive the *person* of The Holy Spirit ('*The* Holy Spirit' or '*Mr* Holy Spirit' if you like) without necessarily experiencing the *release of the Holy Spirit's empowering* in our lives and ministries.

I recently discovered that a former Dean of St Paul's Cathedral came to the same conclusion! (He wrote, the reader might be interested to know, *before* the Welsh and Pentecostal revivals of the twentieth century).

The Dean, the Very Revd J. Armitage Robinson, was a well known scholar. In his commentary on *St Paul's Epistle to the Ephesians*,[7] he says the word Spirit in chapter 1:17 is used in its strictest sense. He points to the fact that Paul is not talking of the Spirit as 'a teachable spirit' (an attitude of mind), but of the Spirit as a teaching Spirit. He then refers to two Gospel passages where the *person* of the Divine Teacher is strongly emphasised:

The Helper, the Holy Spirit whom the Father will send in My name, will teach you everything and make you remember all that I have told you';[8] [and] When, however, the Spirit comes, who reveals the truth about God, He will lead you into all truth.[9]

Robinson continues: 'There in the Greek [in the Gospel passages] we have the definite article: here in Ephesians [1:17] it is absent . . .'

His conclusion is that a distinction may often be rightly drawn in the New Testament between the usage of the word *with* the definite article, and its usage *without it*. With the article, very generally, the word indicates the personal Holy Spirit; without it some special manifestation or bestowal of the Holy Spirit is signified. And this latter is clearly meant in Ephesians 1:17

'A special gift of the Spirit for a special purpose is the subject of St Paul's request' explains Robinson. 'The Spirit thus specially given will make them wise. He will come as the "Spirit of wisdom". Yet more, as the "Spirit of revelation", He will lift the veil, and show them the secret of God.'[10]

The Dean of St Paul's says Paul is asking God to give 'a threefold knowledge embracing all eternity – the past, the future, and not least the present'.[11] He also asks the reader to note (verse 19) that Paul uses not just *one* 'power' word, but four in quick succession – the Greek words *dunamis, energeia, kratos and ischus*. Paul does so, Robinson believes, to hammer home the truth that it is God's supernatural power Paul is asking God to release into people's ministries!

Many ask what relevance this has for you and me? Plenty! I can explain it best by telling you something of John Wesley's testimony. Born and brought up in an Anglican vicarage in the 18th Century, he was snatched from death when the original vicarage burnt down. As a result, his mother believed God had something special in store for John's future.

Many know of him. Most Methodists could tell you what happened to him on May 24th, 1738. It changed his life. But virtually no one can tell you what changed his whole ministry. In fact it's more than that – it's almost as if a conspiracy of silence shrouds that second event. Why? What was it that happened? Why do we not hear about it today?

This is not something insignificant. The conspiracy of silence not only concerns Wesley. Down through the centuries it has effectively snuffed out the amazing experiences of the Spirit's power in other Anglicans, Methodists, Baptists, Lutherans, Presbyterians, Salvation Army officers, Roman Catholics, as well as many of the great Saints of history. Why?

Let me tell you something of John Wesley's story, and perhaps you will understand.

Like all good Anglicans, he was baptized (and received the Holy Spirit, as the Church teaches) as an infant. He received the Holy Spirit at his confirmation as a teenager when the Bishop laid hands on him. After attending university, John was ordained into the Anglican Ministry. As he was priested, the Bishop and clergy laid hands on him and prayed for him *to receive the Holy Spirit* for the office and work of a priest. With all that anointing of the Spirit he should have been well equipped.

After his ordination, John went to a Mission field that was still opening up – in what we now know as the USA. He did not last long as a missionary. After three years he described his ministry as a total failure, and seriously questioned the validity of God's call upon him to the ministry. He had brought no one to Christ. He saw no point in continuing, and took ship back to England.

On the voyage back all on board nearly perished in a hurricane. In imminent danger of sinking, all were called on to pray for their preservation, John with them. But during the storm John was amazed to see one group of men who seemed to be rejoicing – unlike all the others on the ship. When the storm blew itself out, John Wesley sought out this group and demanded a reason for their extraordinary behaviour at the height of the storm. They turned out to be a group of Moravians, and they explained the reason. Because of their assurance in their salvation, the storm held no fears for them. If they perished they would, as they saw it, simply be getting to heaven that much sooner than expected, and that excited them! But it angered Wesley – he had been trying all his life to be good enough for God but had no assurance that if he died he would go to Heaven. And he could only see the Moravians' assurance as one of extraordinary arrogance in thinking they *were* good enough . . . !

But, equally, Wesley could not erase the picture of their joy at the height of the storm from his mind! He pondered over it hard and long and met, and talked the issue out, with anyone who might be able to explain the Moravian standpoint.

And then came May 24th, 1738. Wesley says of the event:

In the evening I went very unwillingly to a society in Aldersgate Street, where one was reading Luther's preface to the Epistle to the Romans. About a quarter before nine, while he was describing the change which God works in the heart through Christ, *I felt my heart strangely warmed*. I felt I did trust in Christ, Christ alone for my salvation: and an assurance was given me, that He had taken away my sins, even mine, and saved me from the law of sin and death. I began to pray with all my might for those who had in a more especial manner despitefully used me and persecuted me. I then testified openly to all there, what I now first felt in my heart'.[12]

The Methodists of the twentieth century may well have heard of that event. In 1988, the 250th Anniversary of the event, many posters

To Reign or Not to Reign

and placards commemorating it reminded us of 'his heart being strangely warmed'. But nothing is ever publicised of another great moment in his life that changed the effectiveness of his ministry! It was simply this. Wesley knew there was something vital missing; if his ministry was to become effective for God, he needed that something. So he set about the search. For the next six months and more, he travelled widely. He visited the Moravians on the continent, and anyone else who might assist him in his quest.

He recognised, in the Church's teaching, that he *had* received the Holy Spirit in baptism, confirmation and ordination – but saw little evidence of it in his ministry. Neither he, nor the Church of his day, saw more than a few of the signs of God's power at work – and yet that power was so transparently present in the New Testament Church.

Then, as suddenly as it was unexpected, the event over which there is such a cloak of silence took place. Wesley records the event in his journal:

> Monday, January 1st, 1739. 'Mr Hall, Kinchin, Ingham, Whitefield, Hutchins, and my brother Charles, were present at our love-feast in Fetter Lane, with about sixty of our brethren. About three in the morning, as we were continuing instant in prayer [they really meant business with God!], the power of God came mightily upon us, insomuch that many cried out for exceeding joy, and many *fell to the ground!* As soon as we were recovered a little from that awe and amazement at the presence of His majesty, [a real Pentecost experience?] we broke out with one voice, 'We praise Thee, O God, we acknowledge Thee to be the Lord.'[13]

It is important to note that this marked a watershed in John Wesley's ministry. George Whitefield's journals speak of the great spiritual awakening which broke upon England and America that same year, 1739 and continued in 1740. It was to be some revival. A bishop of the Church of England had at that time pronounced that the state of the nation was such – utterly lawless, ungodly, much given to vile language, drink, debauchery and the like – that he predicted Christianity in England would cease to exist within a generation!

But the amazing ministries of Wesley, Whitefield and the like – over the next fifty years – would totally reverse, not only that prediction, but the spiritual health of the nation as well.

George Whitefield, whose ministry started at the age of twenty-two in 1737, a couple of years or so after John Wesley's, crossed the Atlantic thirteen times in his amazing thirty-four year ministry, and was known as 'the Apostle of the English empire'! He held crowds of 20,000 spellbound at Moorfields and Kennington Common, London, and in Boston, Massachusetts. Referred to as 'the most extraordinary man of our times' (Lord Bolingbroke) and 'unrivalled in eloquence' (Earl of Chesterfield), he and John Wesley took the UK by storm during most of the remainder of the eighteenth century – yet were often reviled and excluded from churches of their own denomination – so godless were their priests!

John Wesley now saw an extraordinary transformation in his ministry. Thousands and thousands would gather to hear him – often in the streets, or out in the fields simply because churches were barred to him. No doubt that too was the Spirit's work, for space within churches would have limited those crowds! And as he preached, vast numbers were convicted of their sinfulness and need to repent. Many literally fell where they stood under the power of the Spirit.

Yet no one will speak of this 'empowering' on the lives of people like John Wesley! Why not? I believe the answer to be very simple. Leaders of the Church who have no personal experience of this empowering (with the supernatural gifts of the Spirit), would find it difficult indeed to speak or teach on the subject with any real conviction. Nor would they be likely to be able to help people enter into the experience.

We all have the Holy Spirit within us – because He is the one who convicts us of sin, and brings us to salvation. But not all have necessarily experienced the release of the Spirit's power in and through our lives. That is what Paul was earnestly praying for the Ephesian Christians in

Ephesians 1:17.

One can use the analogy of building a house. When complete and correctly wired, and wonderfully equipped with all the electrical gadgetry one could wish to have, none of the electrical equipment is of any use *until the electricians connect the house to the mains power supply!*

To think of another illustration, most of us know something about the workings of a power station. To generate power one needs not only a turbine, but the water to drive it. A power station can look extremely impressive with row upon row of gleaming turbines. But until water is allowed to pass through them, they are actually totally useless, unable to fulfil their function or potential!

Similarly, it doesn't matter how many degrees a minister or priest has when he leaves Theological College, because without tapping into God's power source, there will be little or no effective ministry in terms of changed lives for God's glory. But of course, once tapped in, nothing is wasted . . .

All of us, as Christians, are like those turbines. We need Holy Spirit 'water' to give those 'turbines' effectiveness. Jesus understood that need. Scripture tells us:

> On the last and most important day of the festival Jesus stood up and said in a loud voice, 'Whoever is thirsty should come to Me and drink. As the Scripture says, "Whoever believes in Me, streams of life-giving water will pour out from his side"'. Jesus said this about the Spirit, which those who believed in Him were going to receive. At that time the Spirit had not yet been given, because Jesus had not been raised to glory.[14]

How much do we know about the background to that very short comment in John's gospel? The festival referred to is the Feast of Tabernacles. And it is in the context of what took place at this Feast that we can best understand why Jesus said what He did.

Every day of the feast the priest would go down in procession to the

Pool of Siloam, fill a gold vessel with water from the pool, and then in great ceremony – with much singing and dancing – carry the vessel back up to the Temple. Once there, the priest would perform a number of seemingly (to us) inexplicable rituals.

First, the water in the gold vessel would be ceremonially poured into a hole in the floor near the altar. Beneath the floor were underground channels that would take the water all the way down to the Brook Kedron, and thence back to the pool of Siloam. What a pointless exercise, we might be tempted to think! But it was a symbolic act. You see, it was accompanied by fervent prayer to God to supply good winter rains to fill the rivers and provide for the crops – the winter harvest being a very important one. But that wasn't all.

The priest would then take another vessel, this time filled with wine, and pour that down the same hole. This too had a deep spiritual meaning. The wine being poured out represented for them the Holy Spirit. The Jews believed that way back in history, their people had once all been filled with the Holy Spirit. But at some time – because of sin and disobedience – they lost that anointing. Some schools of rabbinic teaching held a theory that it was when Adam and Eve left the Garden of Eden; others that it was lost at the Tower of Babel; others when they made the golden calf in the wilderness; . . . and so on.

Since that event only the occasional prophet, priest or king received this anointing. And for these last four hundred years before Christ's birth – since the time of Malachi – there had been little or no sign of any anointing on anyone. Not too many were yet aware of what had happened in the immediate past to Zechariah, Mary, Elizabeth, Joseph, Simeon, John the Baptist, Jesus . . .

But they had long remembered Joel's wonderful promise from God: 'Afterwards I will pour out My Spirit on everyone: your sons and daughters will proclaim My message; your old men will have dreams, and your young men will see visions. At that time I will pour out My Spirit even on servants, both men and women'.[15] The awesome prediction of that prophecy is that no one, not even servants or slaves, not even women or children, will be excluded from receiving the anointing.

So we return to the Temple at the Feast of Tabernacles – with the wine in the vessel being poured into the hole. It too would find its way down through those channels to the brook Kedron. And the prayer that accompanied it, year in and year out, at every feast of Tabernacles was simply: 'God, may this be the time You pour out Your Spirit, in abundance, on everyone who longs for that anointing.'

And then it happened! Jesus interrupts the ceremony by shouting: '"If any one is thirsty [for this anointing of the Holy Spirit] let him come to Me . . . whoever believes in Me, streams of life-giving water will pour out from his innermost being . . ." He said this about the Spirit . . . those . . . were going to receive'.[16]

Can you imagine how startled, even shocked, everyone, not least the priest, would have been at that interruption?

But what he shared was of the greatest significance. What He was saying, in essence, was: 'Perhaps all your lives you have longed for the anointing of the Holy Spirit. Well, I am the fulfilment of all that you have been longing for! So come to Me and drink . . . and receive . . .'

One can imagine the response, in the middle of one of our Sunday services, if someone stood up at the back of the church and rudely interrupted the smooth orderly flow of the service by shouting out . . . 'Come to *me* if you want the answers . . . !'

Do we long, deep within our being, for just such an anointing? A longing, if we haven't already done so, to experience the wonderful supernatural gifts listed by Paul in 1 Corinthians 12?

> The Spirit gives one person a message full of wisdom, while to another person the same Spirit gives a message full of knowledge. One and the same Spirit gives faith to one person, while to another person He gives the power to heal ['gifts of healing' in most translations]. The Spirit gives one person the power to work miracles; to another, the gift of speaking God's message [prophecy]; and to yet another, the ability to tell the difference between gifts that come from the Spirit and those that do not

[discernment of spirits]. To one person He gives the ability to speak in strange tongues, and to another He gives the ability to explain [interpret] what is said. But it is *one and the same Spirit* who does all this; as He wishes, He gives a different gift to each person.[17]

There are other 'lists' of gifts given in Scripture. In Ephesians there are the gifts of apostles, prophets, evangelists, pastors and teachers. Their primary purpose is to equip all God's people for ministry.[18] In a letter of Peter we are told about speaking and serving gifts.[19] In Paul's letter to the Romans, there is a long and fairly comprehensive list of gifts.[20] But most of these gifts differ in nature from the list given in Paul's first letter to the Corinthians.[21] The latter are all supernatural, or specially God-given, gifts. The others, by and large, are to do with natural gifts – gifts with which we are born. These gifts must be surrendered to God when we become Christians, asking God to anoint them for His glory – not ours. They are dangerous gifts if not surrendered to God. And there is a further danger.

Even when handed over to God, it is still all too easy to slip back into using them 'in the natural' for our glory, for our purposes, and not His. So Paul puts all this into perspective when he commences this section on natural gifts with the words:

> I urge you therefore, brethren, by the mercies of God, to present your bodies [yourself, your natural gifts, everything that you are] a *living sacrifice*, acceptable to God, which is your spiritual service of worship. And do not be conformed to this world, but be transformed by the renewing of your mind, that you may prove what the will of God is, that which is good, and acceptable and perfect.[22]

But the 1 Corinthians 12 passage on gifts is unique in that it speaks of supernatural, not natural, gifts. We are not born with such gifts. Some are not difficult to recognise: gifts of healing, working of miracles, prophetic utterances, speaking in tongues, interpretation of tongues, and discernment of spirits. The immediate reaction to that might be: 'Fine! But what about gifts like wisdom and knowledge? Surely those are natural gifts?'

However the gift of knowledge referred to here is a gift of knowledge which is quite distinct from the knowledge we understand and accumulate through life by learning or experience. The supernatural gift is a direct revelation of God. How are we to understand that?

Someone requiring prayer for healing, for instance, will usually describe the symptoms they have, such as headache, stomach pain, or whatever. The group can pray for those to be taken away. But to be really effective, they need to know *the root cause* of what is observed or experienced. Let me use a simple illustration.

We were praying for someone virtually unknown to us. The symptoms the person experienced were persistent stomach pains. What we did as a group, as we started to pray for him, was to silently pray in tongues for 'knowledge' (that God alone could reveal to us by His Spirit) to identify the root cause of the pain. The person had been receiving medical treatment, but the medication didn't seem to be having any lasting effect. What God revealed to a person in the group was this: the person was living in an adulterous relationship. No doubt the conflict and anxiety caused the symptoms. This knowledge was unknown to any in the group. And when it was revealed to the person in question (in private), he was 'knocked for six'. He was stunned that God could make this known and it gave him a new understanding of this God he had previously given little more than lip service; and that this God, despite his sin and fall from grace, cared enough for him personally to directly involve Himself in his life in this way! And so he was challenged to repent, and sever that relationship.

This brings us to the next supernatural gift...wisdom. Clearly in the example I have given, the knowledge we were given would be dynamite if used in the wrong way. That is why Paul is at such pains to emphasise that the gifts are to be exercised in love.[23] Thus in a case like this, the knowledge must not to be made public. The person involved must be taken on one side, and asked if what has been revealed might be true in their situation.[24]

It is very important to realise that it is possible, with a word of knowledge, to get the root cause right (i.e. the adultery), but impute it to the wrong person! For example, the person with the stomach ache might reveal he/she is not the guilty party, but is deeply, and secretly, hurt and anxious because his/her spouse is having an affair! So checking at every point, in total confidence, is essential.

In the operation of any gift it is all too easy to be fallible and get it wrong sometimes. For this reason, Paul warns the church to always test the gifts. No wonder the one gift Solomon realised he needed more than any other was the supernatural gift of wisdom. We can't go far wrong in recognising our need of it, and in asking God for that gift.

The one supernatural gift we have not yet looked at is faith. It is not so much a gift for building up one's own faith – although I am sure it does that, too, in some measure. Rather it is a specific gift given to an individual to build up faith in others. It may reveal itself through speakers, writers, preachers, and those who encourage others in their walk of faith.

Paul draws attention to the fact it is one and the same Spirit who works through these God-given gifts. Furthermore, it is as He wishes that He gives different gifts to each person.[25] All the gifts, natural and supernatural, are equally important. All are necessary for the welfare and building up of the whole Body of Christ – His Church![26]

NOTES:
[1] Eph. 1:19b,20
[2] Eph. 1:13
[3] Eph. 1:15,16a
[4] Eph. 1:16b
[5] Eph. 1:17b–20
[6] For a full explanation of this phenomenon, see *Rain in a Dry Land* Pages 75–77
   e.g. '*The* Holy Spirit' Matt. 3:16;4:1; Mark 1:10,12; Luke 2:26;4:1b; John 1:32,33a,14:26; Acts 1:8;2:38;13:2;19.6. Eph. 1:13; Thess. 4:8
   e.g. 'Holy Spirit' Matt. 1:18,20;3:11; Mark 1:8; Luke 1:15,17,35,41;2:25;4:1a;11:13 John 1:33b;20:22. Rom. 9:1 Eph. 1:17

To Reign or Not to Reign

[7] *St Paul's Epistle to the Ephesians* Very Revd J. Armitage Robinson, published by Macmillan, 1904
[8] John 14:26
[9] John 16:13
[10] ibid. see pages 38,39
[11] ibid. see page 40
[12] John Wesley's Journals – May 24th, 1738
[13] ibid : January 1st, 1739
[14] John 7:37–38
[15] Joel 2:28–29
[16] John 7:39
[17] 1 Cor. 12:8–11
[18] See Eph. 4:11–16
[19] See 1 Pet. 4:7–11
[20] See Rom. 12:1–21
[21] See 1 Cor. 12:8–10
[22] Rom. 12:1–2 (*New American Standard Bible*)
[23] See 1 Cor. 13
[24] cf. Gen. 9:22
[25] See 1 Cor. 12:11
[26] see 1 Cor. 12:12–27; 14:12; 14:26–33

Chapter 17

THE CHALLENGE OF THE FAMILIAR

It was after a session of praying for a group of people to be baptized, or drenched in, or released in the gifts of the Holy Spirit when Alfred, a priest, got up and walked out of the room. In the doorway he said he wouldn't be returning. As a linguist he knew a language when he heard one; and these tongues he was hearing around the room were not languages, but something people were making up. He left a very angry man. His wife with two other members of his church felt duty-bound to leave with him. They themselves had all been given a new prayer language in tongues, and were ecstatic with joy. But they had to repress all that as Alfred drove them home. Apparently little was said on the journey home. How do you gainsay your very angry pastor, even when one of you is his wife?

Twice I have had people shout 'Rubbish!' in the middle of a sermon. Each of these incidents led to a good Christian relationship and a deeper understanding of our faith . . . *in the course of time!* Those brave people with the courage to verbalize their anger, had their eyes opened to new insights. Our shared experiences brought them to a deeper, closer, more personal and joyous walk with their Lord.

The same has been true for others who might not have had the sort of boldness to publicly express their disagreement as those already mentioned, but did so in other ways! Some left the church without ever saying why . . . others bottled up their anger and seethed for a season . . . others poured out their complaints to others, and left me to guess.

To Reign or Not to Reign

Every minister of the Gospel can relate to all these and to the pain and sadness that such moments bring. Jesus was often provocative, and He too experienced those who turned away and no longer followed Him.[1] So we stand in good company.

But thankfully, many have later expressed appreciation for those challenges to preconceived and firmly held convictions. The Holy Spirit has to breathe death into everything that is not of God.[2] Only then can new life and understanding, together with God-centred and God-induced convictions, evolve from the ashes of all that was applicable to self. All through our lives we see, as Paul describes it, through a glass darkly; so in many ways, and through many people, we are continually challenged to re-evaluate previous convictions in the light of new understandings.

I first met Alfred, a clergyman, when I was invited to preach for a special occasion, by another vicar, in a village church. As so often happens when a guest preacher is invited, the local vicar had invited all the neighbouring clergy and their parishioners, so there was a very full church. In the course of the sermon I mentioned 'the miracle' connected with the storm at Lynne's sports day.

When coffee was served Alfred made a beeline for me. He was clearly irritated. In a loud voice he told me what he thought of the incident. He argued that God wouldn't involve Himself in the world like that. If He did, he said, what appalling chaos would ensue if everyone was to ask for something different! I tried to explain that no one had gone without rain – just the timing of it had changed! Such phenomena are seen throughout the ministry of Jesus and in many other biblical experiences. They are an expression of God's love for us and the willingness to respond to something Jesus clearly promised: the Father will give you anything you ask for in My name.

Alfred just became more heated. His wife kept suggesting they go home! He finally went. I realised I had done nothing to convince him or meet him where he was.

When I said goodbye to the local vicar a little later, he mentioned a course we ran on 'Practical Experience of the Gifts of the Holy Spirit' and asked if he and his wife could enrol for the next one. His lay reader chipped in and asked if he might come as well. I said I would be delighted. As an afterthought, I asked the vicar to extend an invitation to Alfred and his wife.

No one was more surprised at Alfred's acceptance than me. He dutifully attended the first four weekly teachings, and we had plenty of discussions both after the sessions, and on the phone.

It was at the fifth weekly meeting that we prayed for people to experience the release of the Spirit's power in their lives. Half way round the room I noticed how angry Alfred seemed, so I left the prayer team to be with him. I said, 'Can I pray with you . . . ?', but before I could suggest praying fairly generally (and non-threateningly!) for his ministry, he exploded: 'NO!' We tried for a while to talk through the things that were 'bugging' him; but it wasn't too long before he got up and left in the manner related at the start of this chapter.

Everyone was amazed when he walked into the room the following Tuesday. People remarked afterwards how changed he looked . . . the belligerence was gone . . . there was such a gentleness about him . . . such a peace . . . a look of such happiness . . .

He asked if he could share something with the group. He apologised for the previous week. Then he explained what had happened the day following the meeting. In the morning he found himself coming face to face with Jesus in a new way . . . in the afternoon it was, he said, like experiencing a resurrection. Such a joy flooded his being. He longed for his wife to get back from work so that he could share this with her . . . and then it happened!

As he lay and wept with joy before the Lord, he heard strange sounds coming from his mouth. He was speaking, but the words or sounds were, to him, totally meaningless. Being a linguist, he found himself trying to analyse the sounds. But because they did not seem to follow any recognisable pattern, he decided that he was making it up. But he continued to both articulate them, and try to analyse them. Then he saw a ticker tape moving before his eyes, the kind used by television newsreaders, and he saw all these 'words' moving along the screen.

Again, while he continued mouthing the 'words', he tried to analyse what he saw on the screen. He decided yet again that he was simply making this language up. For instance, some words/symbols seemed to repeat themselves too often for a normal language.

Then he turned to his Bible, and it opened to a chapter in Isaiah. He saw in that chapter the kind of repetition he didn't expect to find in a language! He realised he was reading the interpretation of his tongue.

Glory to God! Or, as John Wesley and his group proclaimed on a similar occasion: 'We praise Thee, O God; we acknowledge Thee to be the Lord'.

Through this course a number of clergy and ministers of various denominations have discovered a new experience of God's empowering in their lives and ministries. So often we hear the same refrain: 'Why weren't we taught this at Bible School/Theological College? If only this had happened to me twenty/thirty/forty years ago – at the beginning of my ministry! What a difference it would have made!'

Devastating as it is, many in leadership suggest such gifts were only for the first century of Christendom, and are now no longer needed. Why deny, for so many, the precious heritage that should be theirs?

Jesus Himself speaks graphically of what that empowering can mean in terms of healing gifts. When the woman with an issue of blood touched Him, Jesus turned round. In spite of the large crowd pushing and shoving all round Him, He asked who had touched Him. 'Everyone denied it, and Peter said, 'Master, the people are all round You and crowding in on You.' But Jesus said, 'Someone touched Me, for I knew it *when power went out of Me.*"[3]

The disciples recognised their need of such gifts. They only had to see Jesus at work to realise how ineffectual their lives had been for God, in comparison to His. And that created a deep longing within them:

> One day Jesus was praying in a certain place. When He had finished one of his disciples said to Him, 'Lord, teach us to pray, just as John taught his disciples.' Jesus said to them, 'When you

The Challenge of the Familiar

pray, say this:
Father:
May Your holy name be honoured;
may Your Kingdom come.
Give us day by day the food we need.
Forgive us our sins
for we forgive everyone who does us wrong.
And do not bring us to hard testing.[4]

One might ask, what has this to do with the longing for spiritual gifts for ministry? The next passage in Scripture explains why. Jesus tells the tale of an imaginary person having to wake up a neighbour in the middle of a night to ask for some bread to feed an unexpected late night guest. But the neighbour is in bed and refuses to answer the door.[5]

Jesus says: 'He will get up and give you everything you need because you are not ashamed to keep on asking. And so I say to you, ask . . . seek . . . knock'; and if you do that *persistently* 'how much more, then, will the Father in Heaven *give the Holy Spirit* to those who ask Him!'[6]

I used to consider the Lord's prayer as a basic everyday prayer. In one sense it is, considering the original request: 'Lord, teach us to pray'[7] But is this what the disciples were actually asking? The answer has to be 'No'! Why?

Very simply, the disciples *knew* how to pray. They were Jews. They would have learnt to pray while still on their mother's knee. Unlike many in Christian circles, an important focal point for worship for Jews is the home. If at no other time, prayer is offered at the weekly sabbath meal celebrated in the family home – week in, and week out. It explains why so many remain true to their Jewish roots even when dispersed far from synagogue or temple. The home was, and is, the family centre of prayer and worship. (If only it were so today in the Christian home – with family breakdown so much a feature of daily life.) So why did they say, 'Lord teach us to pray'?

To understand the reason for the question, we have to understand something about Jesus' own ministry. It didn't matter what question was asked of Him, He always *discerned* 'the hidden agenda' in any question put to Him. He always '*knew*', if you like, where the questioner really 'itched'! And so it is here.

The disciples' question has to do with a common problem familiar to all. All have experienced it. It concerns seemingly ineffective or unanswered prayer. How many times have you found yourself asking, 'Why doesn't God answer my prayer?' or 'Why did God allow this to happen?'

The disciples were no different. But in observing Jesus, they could not have been unaware how much time He spent in prayer. Often it would be a long time before dawn when He disappeared to prepare for the day in prayer. Equally frequently, after times of ministry, He would go away and pray again – as He did, for example, after the feeding of the five thousand.

What they could not overlook were *the results*! They saw the miracles, the healing and deliverance of so many, and so much else – all in great profusion and variety.

No surprise then, if one unwraps what the disciples left unsaid, that their plea was: 'Lord, teach us to pray as You do, so that we too will see effective answers to prayer!' Surely it is true for us?

In this anecdote, Jesus clearly links the 'ability to pray' request of the disciples to their need for 'Holy Spirit' empowering. 'Then will the Father in heaven give [the] "Holy Spirit" [power] to those who ask Him,'[8] says Jesus. Looking at the Lord's Prayer in that light, reveals some costly challenges.

The prayer itself can be divided into four main sections or topics The first section is:
i) 'Father: May Your holy name be honoured;
   May Your Kingdom come,
   May Your will be done.'[9]

What Jesus clearly indicates is that if one really longs for that 'empowering', it is essential to declare exactly where one stands. Whatever we ask for in prayer, firstly: God is to receive all the honour.

The Challenge of the Familiar

not John Knight, or Joe Soap. The temptation, however cleverly we disguise it, is to want glory or fame for ourselves. We all, at some time, crave the praise and adulation of others; to be considered a success with a powerful, effective ministry; to be the leader of a church that draws crowds ... Let's be honest, the temptation to receive any praise that's going is an ever present reality!

Equally, it must be *HIS* kingdom (His will done) that is established. You can see the kind of danger faced by Tele-evangelists of the USA and elsewhere! If you have that special 'something', that charismatic gift, whatever it may be, then beware, says Jesus. Are you quite sure it is *GOD'S* Kingdom we are bent on establishing?

ii) The second point Jesus emphasises for those who seek the Spirit's empowering is this:

'Give us day by day the food we need'.[10]

And, yes, it does refer to a need for our bodily requirements to be met. If we are not fit and healthy, we are not going to be very profitable servants in His Kingdom service. But it also applies, even more importantly, to our spiritual requirements.

Take Jesus as an example. He did nothing, He said nothing, He tells us, *unless* the Father told Him to do it or say it. Now that speaks of an extraordinarily close relationship between Him and His Father. It is borne out, in His three brief years of ministry, in the time He spent 'apart in prayer', in His amazing knowledge and comprehension of Scripture, and of His role within it.

What Jesus wants us to know is this: if we would like that empowering, then it requires us to centre our lives on a moment by moment 'living relationship' with the Father. Paul understood exactly what Jesus was getting at. In his prayer for the Ephesian Christians, he prayed they would receive Holy Spirit empowering to 'make [them] wise and reveal God to [them], so that [they] will know Him'.[11] That requires much time spent in prayer; much time in worship; much time in the study of Scripture; but also, more than anything else, much time spent alone with God seeking His leading and direction.

'It is easier', wrote Oswald Chambers, 'to serve God without a vision, easier to work for God without a call, because then you are not bothered by what God requires; common sense is your guide, veneered over with Christian sentiment . . .'[12]

We are well aware of our human failings. The busier we are, the more likely we are to spend more and more time being busy *for* God, and less and less time *with* God; and prayer, study of the Word and waiting on God are no longer the top priority in our lives. So much time in prayer is taken up with speaking *to* God – rather than hearing what *He* has to say to *us*! Unless we are careful, we are past masters at suggesting what is needed, presenting Him with our long shopping lists, or presenting *our* plans for Him to bless!

What really delights the heart of God is a person who does what is pleasing to God.

The third important aspect Jesus refers to is this:

iii) 'Forgive us our sins, for we forgive everyone who does us wrong'.[13]

Yes, we can only expect forgiveness from God in so far as we are prepared to forgive those who have wronged us. But there is also an essential spiritual principle here we all too easily overlook.

Many hoping to move on spiritually with God, still have unforgiving or unrepentant hearts, even bitterness or hatred, towards people who have hurt or abused them in the past. How many times I hear people discuss relationships that are a mess and look upon them as impossible to resolve. So what do they do? Very often the easy option is to ignore them and, as they might say, just go on with God instead.

Experience proves many still bear grudges, still deal bitterly or censoriously with others – while professing to love and serve God. Jesus simply says we can't do this. We cannot shut the door on all past failures in relationships, and hope they will just go away!

All that accumulated garbage – bitterness, pain, hurt – sets up blockages *within us* that actually *prevent the Holy Spirit's power working effectively* through us.

On the evening of the first Easter day, Jesus said: 'Peace be with you. As the Father sent Me, so I send you'. Here was His commissioning. He followed it by breathing on them and saying, 'Receive [the] Holy

Spirit'.[14]

Jesus specifically refers to the need for 'Holy Spirit *empowering*' rather than asking for the *person* of the Holy Spirit to indwell them.

Forty days later, at the Ascension, Jesus said to them 'Do not leave Jerusalem, but wait for the gift I told you about, the gift My Father promised . . . [for] . . . when the Holy Spirit comes upon you, you will be filled with power . . .'[15] Clearly they only received *this* 'empowering' fifty days after Easter: 'When the day of Pentecost came . . . they were all filled with Holy Spirit . . .'[16]

One explanation for the apparent non-reception of Holy Spirit empowering on Easter Day is the anointing would have to wait until after Jesus was glorified. At a Feast of Tabernacles some time before, when Jesus claimed to be the baptizer in the Holy Spirit, we are told: 'At that time the Spirit had not yet been given, because Jesus had not been raised to glory'.[17] Similarly, at an earlier event on Easter day when Jesus had met with Mary Magdalene in the garden, He had said to her: "Do not hold on to Me because I have not yet gone back up to the Father'.[18]

But I believe there is another explanation that makes sense.

When the disciples had previously asked Jesus for this gift, Jesus gave them a prayer that established the kind of life they would be expected to live. And, in particular, they would have to deal with all the blockages caused by broken relationships in the past.

Now – when Jesus breathed on them and said 'Receive Holy Spirit [*power*]', he followed it up with something identical: 'If you forgive people's sins, they are forgiven; if you do not forgive them, they are not forgiven'! Traditionally, in some parts of the Christian church, this is seen as the authority that allows priests to hear confessions and – even more important – the right to forgive, or not forgive sins, in Jesus' name as the case may be.

Surely there is another aspect to this. Was not Jesus saying to the disciples: this empowering will be yours, but you still have to deal with this issue of past 'spoilt' relationships. If you forgive people's sins, those things they have done to hurt or abuse you, then they are forgiven; but, if *YOU* do not forgive them, they are NOT forgiven. And that 'retained garbage' will continue to be a hindrance to the empowering you seek; and you will not be a clear channel for God's grace to minister healing to others, or to operate the other gifts of the Spirit.

Taking that into consideration, we are reminded that on the day of the Ascension Jesus says: Do not leave Jerusalem until you receive the power of the Holy Spirit. Note what follows next. 'The apostles went back to Jerusalem' as ordered, and 'up to the room where they were staying', and during the next ten days 'gathered frequently to pray as a group, together with the women and with Mary the mother of Jesus and with His brothers'.[19] Jesus had impressed on them not only the need to ask God's forgiveness, but to forgive all those who had wronged them.

To return to 'The Lord's Prayer', we need to consider the final part of that prayer:

iv) 'And do not bring us to hard testing'.

Let's not mince matters here. If the power of God begins to work through us in an increasing number of ways, temptations will begin to threaten us from every side. There will be the temptation to boast of 'my' gifts; to capitalize on those gifts for self-aggrandizement (Note the TV Evangelists and so many others who have grown rich, and abused such power). There will be a temptation to manipulate power for my own ends; to make myself a focal point of praise and adulation; even to use the wealth acquired to win praise as a public benefactor . . . Money begets power, power corrupts, and absolute power corrupts absolutely!

Does that infer one should shy away from such gifts? Jesus charges us to get our priorities right – God, and His kingdom, are to be central to everything we do, think, or say! His *super*natural empowering gifts are for *His* glory and the salvation of many.

So Jesus urges us to go on, and on, and on *asking*, and *seeking*, and *knocking* until we receive that empowering and the gifts we need for ministry. He warns us not to give up simply because nothing seems to happen for a while. Remember the man in bed trying to get some sleep? (what a delightfully humorous picture of God!): He '*will* get up and give you everything you need because you are not ashamed to keep on, and on, and on asking'.

There is a final point Jesus makes in response to the disciples' request for empowering: there will always be those who are fearful that if they ask for supernatural gifts they might get Satan's counterfeit gifts.

Don't be concerned about that, Jesus tells them:

Would any of you who are fathers give your son a snake when he asks for fish? Or would you give him a scorpion when he asks for an egg? Bad as you are, you know how to give good things to your children. How much more, then, will the Father in Heaven give [the] Holy Spirit to those who ask Him.[20]

NOTES:

[1] John 6:66
[2] Isa. 40:7 (See Chapter 3 for amplification on this passage)
[3] Luke 8:45–48
[4] Luke 11:1–4
[5] Luke 11:5-8a
[6] Luke 11:9–13
[7] Luke 11:1b
[8] Luke 11:13
[9] Luke 11:2
[10] Luke 11:3
[11] Eph. 1:17b
[12] Oswald Chambers in *My Utmost for His Highest* (See March 4)
[13] Luke 11:4a
[14] John 20:21–22
[15] Acts 1:4b,8
[16] Acts 2:1a,4a
[17] John 7:39
[18] John 20:17
[19] Acts 1:12–14
[20] Luke 11:11–13

Chapter 18

'THE PROOF OF THE PUDDING . . .' or

'GOD ANSWERS PRAYER – ASK TRACY'

Dawn, now married, was a member of a previous congregation. She grew up in a Baptist Manse and had known and loved the Lord for some time. One Sunday night while praying for people's specific needs, Dawn's deep concern was for her work environment. She had a problem with which many of us are all too familiar, the lack of courage and wisdom to share her faith with people with whom she worked. She believed she had, in a sense, denied Christ by remaining silent on many occasions when she should have spoken up. So, just as the disciples had done when ordered never again to speak of Jesus, we prayed God would give her that gift of boldness[1] and the wisdom to share sensitively.

A few weeks later Tracy, a colleague of Dawn's at work, spoke to all the office staff of how upset she was. Her sister's child had been rushed to hospital critically ill, and the doctors were unsure why. To add to that, her father had just been made redundant. The advice given by fellow members of staff was all contrary to what a Christian could accept: what you need to do is to consult the stars, and so on. Dawn found herself no longer able to remain silent, and spoke to the girl of what she believed Jesus could do. A little later the same day, just as she was going off on holiday, Dawn promised Tracy she would pray for her sister's child, and her father. Tracy was very appreciative of that, and thanked her.

Returning from holiday, Tracy greeted Dawn with the news that the baby had totally recovered, and the doctors were unable to explain the sudden turn around. What was more, her father had found another job! What thrilled Dawn most of all was the effect all this had on the other members of staff in her office. After that incident, if asked what to do when things go wrong, staff have been overheard to say, 'God answers prayer – ask Tracy!'

God also reveals in Scripture that He is able to intervene and provide childless couples with the child they so long for. When angelic visitors told Abraham that this time next year his wife Sarah would have a child, Sarah (who was far too old to have one) was overheard laughing in her tent at the impossibility of the suggestion.[2] Yet, just as promised, Sarah conceived the child she and Abraham had waited for all their married lives.

The same happened to Hannah, the mother of Samuel, another miracle baby;[3] and to Zechariah and Elizabeth with the birth of John the Baptist. And God continues to do these things.

Linda and Ken were going through a particularly difficult time. For quite a number of years they had longed for a child, but without success. As Linda said: 'It is difficult to describe the emotional pain that accompanies childlessness . . . crunch point arrived with yet another friend's pregnancy. I couldn't believe how I felt about it – devastated. It was the start of both my marriage and other relationships being affected. Pain can be destructive, and I felt at its mercy. My cries to God were desperate and I knew I had to learn to accept what seemed a bitter pill, or my life would dissolve to nothing . . . I knew God was in this with us and I had to hang on to that, no matter how things turned out. One evening in October 1988, I had a long chat with the Lord and decided to write it down. I don't think I've experienced such intimacy since. The following is only part of it:

'How do I live with this pain, Lord?'

'Give it to Me,' He said.

'Lord, waiting to conceive is harder than waiting to give birth.'

'I know,' He said. 'I waited a long time before allowing My Son to be born in the fullness of time. I grieved over it, over man's inability to grasp My love for him, and what I wanted to do for him through My

'The Proof of the Pudding . . .' or 'God Answers Prayer – Ask Tracy'

Son.'

In the course of this conversation I felt the Lord was assuring me I *would* have a child, but totally lost sight of this in the months following, such was the pain . . .'

Later, the hospital prescribed a three-month course of Clomid. But at the end of that period there was no result. Linda and Ken then happened to come on one of our Holy Spirit courses with their house group. During each week of the course we would spend time praying through this with Linda and Ken, sometimes as a couple, sometimes individually. On one of those evenings I came home and shared with Jill that I believed the Lord showed me quite clearly Linda would soon conceive. Jill confirmed that she had the same understanding. Later that same week, while counselling Linda, Jill told her of the assurance we both had. I believe it is part of that necessary step of faith to nail one's colours to the mast when given such assurance. Of course it is not easy to do, but 'faith is to be sure of the things we hope for, to be certain of the things we cannot see. It was by their faith [believing in, and acting on, what they understood God had revealed to them] that people of ancient times won God's approval'.[5] God often waits for *us* to step out in faith before He takes the next step!

That assurance was given to Linda at the end of May 1989. In August of the same year Linda found she was pregnant, and little Samuel was born on the 11th April 1990.

Linda's testimony brought Hannah's story, in the Book of Samuel, vividly and painfully alive for me. Remember how Hannah longed for a child for so many years, with the taunts of Penninah constantly ringing in her ears? In her deep distress, she cried bitterly to the Lord, and the prophet Eli accused her of being drunk: 'No, I'm not drunk, sir,' she answered. 'I haven't been drinking! I am desperate, and I have been praying, pouring out my troubles to the Lord. Don't think I am a worthless woman. I have been praying like this because I'm so miserable'.[6]

And God heard her prayer, and Samuel was conceived in her womb!

Linda concludes her testimony with these words: 'Did *God* give me this child or was it the result of the previous course of drugs? What can appear to be a conflict is not – if one's perception is of a God "in all and who knows all" . . . God still requires us to take a decision of faith in His ability to handle our lives. In the years of childlessness, I found the hardest test that of trusting God. And I'm not sure I did a very good job; but even in my failure He loved me. He taught me more about Himself and myself through a process of pain and co-operation with Him. He is sovereign'.

These things didn't only happen in Biblical times – God's promise to us is that He never changes.

Another series of answers to prayer were given to Mary, another member of our Emmanuel congregation. Mary had a heart problem that developed when her third child was born in 1968. It was not life threatening, but a nuisance because capacity for physical activities was greatly diminished, and occasionally resulted in unconsciousness for brief periods of time. The attacks could be controlled with drugs, and Mary was told she would have to take them for the rest of her life. But the attacks increased over the years, and in more recent times she had also experienced pain with these attacks. The symptoms eventually became so distressing that a visit to a cardiac specialist resulted in the decision that she needed by-pass surgery.

The day she learnt this, 2nd March 1989, Mary turned up at our Holy Spirit course very flushed and uncomfortable looking. No longer was she able to walk the half-mile to the shops without having to stop and take a break; nor could she dig the garden, or ride her bicycle. As she explained all this, together with the disconcerting news from the specialist, we suggested prayer for healing. She readily agreed.

Within a very short time Mary's colour had returned to normal. By the end of the evening as she herself recorded it:

'. . . I felt the most tremendous sense of peace come over me. My chest seemed bathed in a warm glow. When I stood up to leave my pulse was steady and strong instead of the fluttering state it had been in for some time, and I felt terrific. From that evening onwards [more than ten years now!] I have not had one pain. I dig in the garden, cycle

'The Proof of the Pudding . . .' or 'God Answers Prayer – Ask Tracy'

vigorously, and take part in all sorts of physical activities'. For those who don't know Mary, she was on the go sixteen hours a day, including keeping pace with a son she taught at home. 'I returned to the hospital for a further stress-test cardiogram, taken while walking on a treadmill, and the cardiac specialist said it was magnificent, and discharged me. I praise and thank God for making me whole'.

Yes, indeed, we do praise God for such miracles. But that's not all there is to Mary's story. Listen to her story as Anne Coomes recorded it.[7]

'Life is a tricky business. You start out with such high hopes. How do things go so terribly wrong? For Mary, adulthood began with an innocent mistake, swelled into a tragedy, and nearly ended with an act of criminal stupidity. For by the autumn of 1988 she seriously considered taking a walk and just never coming back. She had had enough of life.

'The youthful mistake was to get married at the age of nineteen to a man she considered Mr Right. Four children later she had to face the fact that he was very much Mr Wrong for her. By then she had learned the old truth that for sheer, sustained misery, you just can't beat an unhappy marriage. The scope for unhappiness is vast with endless rows, bitter recriminations, constant suspicions, and abusive language. All in the comfort of your own home.

'The tragedy happened in 1974. Mary's mother, to whom she was much attached, couldn't sleep one night, and sat up late making some stuffed animals for a charity stall. In the early hours she banked down the coal fire and went to bed. The firemen could only surmise what happened next: a spark flew out of the banked fire and landed on the pile of inflammable materials. Within minutes the room was an inferno. The flames spread. Mary's mother and stepfather died in the fire.

'"I was devastated", said Mary. Only the need to care for four young children kept her going at all. "That and God. I hoped that somehow my parents had gone to be with Him. I knew they certainly believed in Him". Her stepfather had been a Methodist lay preacher.

'Mary believed in God too, and had been attracted by Christ ever since she had seen the film *The Robe* as a teenager. "I knew that

Christians lived by high moral standards, and had tried very hard to live that way too, to please God. But I had very limited success, and after many attempts had despaired. I could only hope that when I came to die one day that God would review my life and say "Well, I guess you meant well, I'll let you into heaven".

'The next few years were no easier at home, and by 1980 Mary's marriage was collapsing. Mary had strongly felt that marriage was a sacred relationship before God, and had returned to church for several months, seeking some sort of help. "I was so desperate for comfort, and also for truth about life. I wanted God, I wanted answers, but I could not seem to get through. I tried to read the Bible, but it was so big, I hardly knew where to start. I could not find God. I did not know how to get to Him." The final ending of marriage made her feel more of a failure than ever.

'She turned for comfort to her boss, and soon he invited her to move in with him over in Duston . . . she revelled in the new found love and comfort, but then felt too guilty to go to her new local church, St Francis. One evening the vicar called on her. She welcomed him in, but wondered if he would be so happy to come in if he knew she was "living in sin". After a friendly chat, he rose to leave with "Well, we'll see you in church then?" Mary decided to risk it: "Oh yes," she said. The people at the new church were very friendly . . . and Mary began to go regularly.

'Then Bob asked her to marry him, and they decided they wanted to have children. So late in the summer of 1980, while still waiting for the divorce . . . Mary went for an operation to reverse her sterility. She was frightened at the thought . . . and mused . . . "Bob, I wish you were a Christian. I could use you in church praying for me right now". To her surprise and delight, Bob readily agreed to go with her to church the Sunday before the operation. Afterwards he said it hadn't been as terribly boring as he had feared, and promised to come on special occasions. By January 1981 Mary was pregnant, and Simon was born that October. It was a slightly tricky situation, as she was not yet free to marry Bob, but again the church said nothing, and Mary continued to attend regularly. She and Bob were married early in 1982 and settled down happily to build a life together. Both began to attend St Francis regularly. Bob even decided to go for confirmation.

Mary's comment was "We both felt very positive about Christianity, though I still had this guilt about everything I'd done wrong in life..."

'The family moved to a new home and a new parish, and found themselves members of Emmanuel Shared Church, Weston Favell. And it was early on in her new life at Southfields that the final major thing went wrong for Mary – "And this time, for once, it was utterly and entirely my own stupid fault." It began when she ran up some bills and rather than tell Bob, she began to borrow money to pay them off. The hitch was, it wasn't money she had any right to borrow in the first place. Then she borrowed some more, and then again some more. "Within months the sum had soared and I had no hope of paying it back. It worried me constantly. If anyone found out, I could face criminal charges. I had never meant this to happen. I could hardly believe it had happened. I was so frightened. I hated myself, I thought if anybody knew what I had done, they would despise me. I felt guilty and condemned all the time. It was ruining my life."

'Her situation was all the more frustrating because the new rector, John Knight, had launched courses to teach the church members how to share their faith, and Mary badly wanted to join these. She had noticed that some of the more radiant Christians in the church had signed up, and she thought she might learn their secret. "I wanted that extra thing they had". So she signed on to join the Evangelism Explosion course, and then felt like a total hypocrite. "I knew so clearly where I wanted to be – a proper Christian, but I was very far away from it and had simply no idea how to get there now."

'By October the crisis had come, and she could bear the strain no longer. She even contemplated suicide. When she finally got up the courage to tell Bob, he was as devastated as she had feared he would be. "The girls tried to comfort me. One bought me a mug with 'I love you' on it. The other bought Bob a mug with 'Cheer up Dad' on one side, and a man holding a gun to his head on the other side! That about summed up Bob's feelings."

'Bob stood by Mary. Together they went . . . and confessed what Mary had done . . . there were no recriminations . . . no threats . . . Bob arranged to return the money . . . a second mortgage on the house ... "One thing they did make clear: they totally forgave me. It was the first time in my life I had ever seen such unselfish and totally Christian reactions. It moved me deeply."

'But her inner guilt remained. Mary despised herself. When the Evangelism Explosion course got under way, Mary felt too unworthy, too guilty. She did not know how to square things with God. Then one night there was a prayer meeting and as Mary sat silent in her misery one of the group, Neville, suddenly paused and said: "I feel God is giving me a message for someone here in the group. I believe it is this: 'Your sins *are* forgiven and you've been washed clean by the blood of the Lamb.' Mary was thunderstruck. "In that instant I suddenly perceived what Christianity was all about. Not *us* doing good to be pleasing to God, *but He* in love reaching out to us, offering us forgiveness. That night I felt God had lifted me out of the mire and given me a fresh start. Years of anxiety and guilt . . . rolled away."

'The following weeks were very trying for Bob. "He was terribly despondent at having to pay back the huge debt that I had run up, and now instead of me creeping about the place all contrite, I was full of joy!" She desperately wanted Bob to share in her newfound relationship with Jesus, and tried to share with him the things she was learning on the evangelism course. It all came to a head one night when Mary had already gone to bed. She had left Bob in the sitting room in a grumpy mood, irritated by all this joy of hers about God. She was sitting in bed praying that the Lord would work in him . . . when the door opened and slowly Bob walked in, got ready for bed, and said, "I'm ready to give my life to the Lord, will you pray with me?" Mary was over the moon. "I just felt so flooded with gratitude to God for giving me so much when I deserved nothing". A real marriage partnership began that night as Mary and Bob together gave themselves and everything they had to God.'[8]

Of course that is not the end of their story. Mary went on to become

'The Proof of the Pudding . . .' or 'God Answers Prayer – Ask Tracy'

the Teacher Trainer responsible for the Evangelism Explosion programme at Emmanuel and later still, accepted for the full time ministry. In marvellous ways Mary also had the added blessing of seeing a grown-up son and a daughter discover the joy of their own salvation through Christ. And so the ripples in the pool extend ever wider . . . and God is glorified in these amazing things He delights to do.

And the joy of it all is that this is no isolated incident. During our ten years at Emmanuel we saw so many families and individuals experiencing wonderful transformations, as well as healing, take place in their lives; Betty and Mike, Karen and William, Jean, Gary; another Mike – so strait-jacketed by a traditionalist Anglicanism that he felt threatened by every aspect of renewal. Then step by gentle step, he was wonderfully released to experience the personal touch and reality of God in so many areas of his life. Shirley and Chris discovering the power of prayer: crippled by the control cigarette smoking had over them, they asked for prayer to be freed of this hold upon their lives – and were instantly released from any desire to smoke any more. And year by year an amazing number of people literally changed, transformed and healed by God's love.

At every conference, and the many courses we have held, we have seen God touching people's lives and bringing healing, forgiveness, restoration and renewal. How gracious God is!

Marion didn't want to come forward to ask for healing. When you have asked, and asked, and seen no result, it is easy for faith to diminish, or to believe that God perhaps expects you to endure stoically and 'learn to live with it'! She had spent all day at an OSL Conference[9] I was speaking at, and the evening celebration as well. The pews were particularly uncomfortable. So when prayer ministry was offered, the last thing Marion wanted was prayer. But her friend was persistent. Marion finally relented, and had to be helped on to the platform. The rheumatoid arthritis was far advanced and affected almost every part of her body – all the joints in arms and hands, legs and feet, as well as the neck and back. She walked with difficulty. A group of us prayed for her.

To Reign or Not to Reign

There were not too many observable signs of change! How many times have you experienced that, or prayed for someone and been disappointed when they respond: 'there doesn't seem to be any change'? Our faith-level barometer takes a depressing dive. 'Why doesn't God answer my/our prayer?' Marion left the platform with equal difficulty, and went home.

After leaving this conference, I went on to the Green Pastures Healing Centre in Bournemouth where I was to lead a week long conference. In the middle of the week Owen Skilleter, wonderfully used in the healing ministry and a chaplain of OSL, dropped in to see me. He told me they had received reports during the week of a number of people who had been healed as a result of our ministry at Immanuel the previous Saturday. He mentioned that one of these was a woman who had been totally healed of rheumatoid arthritis! There was much rejoicing at Green Pastures, and I believe the news of these acts of healing did much to raise the faith level there, and we saw some remarkable healings. But when one hears news like that, without actually seeing the person concerned, it all seems a bit remote. And, yes! Isn't there just the teeniest questioning as to how genuine the healing was? We all understand that. It's the natural human reaction to any significant sign of God at work. We find ourselves asking (doubts trying to surface!) can it really be true? By the time I left Bournemouth, I still had no direct contact with Marion herself to confirm or deny the story. I learnt she lived in a village some way outside Bournemouth, but quite where no one seemed to know. I heard no more for four months.

I was again in the Bournemouth area conducting a renewal weekend, this time for the Canford Heath United Reformed Church.[10] I was on the point of starting the first talk on the Saturday morning when three or four women scrambled into some seats near the back. I knew they must be strangers to the church because the 'greeters' at the door clearly didn't know them!

At the tea break, one of the latecomers came over and introduced herself. It turned out to be Marion, the person who had been totally healed of arthritis! Later in the day I persuaded her to give her testimony.

'The Proof of the Pudding . . .' or 'God Answers Prayer – Ask Tracy'

She told us that when she finally got home to her village that night four months previously, she had been able to jump out of the car and literally run up the steps to her house. Having to stop at the top, puffing and panting, she realised that although she was healed, she still had to contend with an out-of-shape seventy-five-year-old body! It was noticeable to all present that although there was still a very slight stiffness around the ankles, there was no sign of any arthritis anywhere else. Isn't God gracious? Alleluia!

God does not only heal or resolve physical issues. Many carry painful hurts and trauma from the past. Inevitably, although one might have great faith in God to heal present situations, many question whether God can do anything about those things that took place way back in the past – the results of being unloved, unwanted, neglected, abused. There are the problems of false guilt and shame. Many of those things have left so many people virtual cripples; and others deeply traumatised psychologically. Can God 'put right' something that took place five, ten, twenty or even sixty years ago? Indeed He can! We have seen a number being healed in these areas too. Let me share just one of them.

Nine years ago Fiona and her family bought a house in an attractive village. They had three beautiful children, and the youngest was about to start playgroup. Let Fiona pick up the story: 'I was very much looking forward to having more time available to get involved with what God was doing in our community. However, when I discovered a few months later that I was pregnant again, I was devastated. Suddenly the future seemed to promise nothing but hard work, and frustration and that I would not be able to give the rest of the family the time and attention they needed.

'Three months of sickness and physical exhaustion made the emotional adjustment even more difficult. Though I struggled to see how God could be in control, I did gradually move through various stages from resentment to resignation, and then to acceptance. Christian friends were a wonderful source of practical support and encouragement. After our son William was born, life very gradually returned to normal again, and we all grew to love and enjoy our new addition, though it took about two years before I fully accepted my loss of freedom and control. I began to see positive outcomes as God opened up new relationships and opportunities as a result. A few years later we moved to the Midlands.'

Later still, Fiona attended a week-end conference we arranged on healing, conducted by Francis and Judith MacNutt,[11] who are internationally known in the Healing ministry. Fiona continues – 'The first session was about forgiveness and healing in relationships. When we were asked to offer our particular concerns to the Lord, my thoughts were with my cousin and her husband who were going through a very difficult time in their marriage. Francis then began to sing in tongues to allow the Holy Spirit to minister to us.

'I was totally unprepared for what happened next as all the pain and struggle I have described above came to the surface – even though I had presumed the issue was long over when God had dealt with my feelings. Suddenly a little window opened before my eyes and the Holy Spirit made me very aware that something was still missing in my relationship with William. There was a gap in his emotional experience. He had missed out on what now seemed essential for every unborn child – the excitement and anticipation of a new baby's arrival. For William this had never happened.

'I knew I needed to go forward for prayer, and joined the queue. A friend, Mary, prayed with me that God would heal the emotional void within William, and also that William would settle and feel absolutely secure in God's love, and the love of his family and friends.

'I arrived home feeling very reassured that God was able to reach back into the past and pinpoint a need of which I was previously unaware. On my way to bed I checked on William. He was sleeping soundly. [William was not present at the evening event, so knew nothing of what had taken place.]

'Next morning I was sitting on my bed when in he came, his little face glowing with delight:

"Mummy, do you know what? I've just been born!"

"Have you, darling", I responded instantly, the Lord enabling me to see the significance of this amazing statement. "We've been looking forward to you coming for so long, and we're excited you're here!"

'I took him in my arms like a new baby. After a cuddle, he asked for a pretend feed at the breast! Over the next few days other evidences of a new security and peace in his inner self were noted. What an incredible God we have! As Judith MacNutt said later in the Conference that same day: "When God created you, He *didn't* make a mistake" – and He didn't make a mistake when he made Willam!'[12]

NOTES:
[1] Acts 4:29
[2] Gen. 18:9–15; 21:1–8
[3] 1 Sam. 1:9–20
[4] Luke 1:13–20, 57–66
[5] Heb. 11:1,2
[6] 1 Sam. 1:15,16 – See also from verse 9.
[7] Anne Coomes, former Communications Officer, Diocese of Peterborough, formerly editor of *CEN*
[8] *Faith in the Diocese of Peterborough – Twelve disciples tell their stories* edited by Anne Coomes (Booklet available from Diocese of Peterborough £1 – with the request it be passed on to someone else, *not* put on your bookshelf!)
[9] OSL – Order of St Luke Conference, Immanuel United Reformed Church, Southbourne, Bournemouth, 6th June 1992
[10] 10th/11th October, 1992
[11] Directors of Christian Healing Ministries Inc. Jacksonville, Florida. Francis is author of the best seller *Healing*, as well as *The Prayer That Heals*, *The Power to Heal* etc.; he and Judith are co-authors of *Praying for your Unborn Child*
[12] Fiona's personal testimony

Chapter 19

CLINGING TO A LAMPPOST AT DAWN

The Holy Spirit draws a variety of reactions from different people. On the day of Pentecost, for instance, some bystanders 'made fun of the believers, saying, "These people are drunk!"' Peter had to put the record straight: 'These people are not drunk, as you suppose; it is only nine o'clock in the morning'.[1]

Many people have difficulty with anything supernatural. For some their immediate inclination is to reject it out of hand. For others it smacks of the paranormal, even if not positively sinister! For yet others it is both questionable and *un*reasonable.

A former Archbishop, Michael Ramsey, who stands at the very heart of orthodox Christian tradition and teaching, is much more open. He says:

It is by 'ruach' [the *now* Word of God] that the prophets prophesy, and the implication is that the Spirit inspires not only the *ecstasy* which they sometimes experience, but the *message* of which they are conscious and the *impulse* to deliver it'.[2] (The emphases are mine)

Scripture explains it like this: 'The Spirit of the Lord shall rest upon him, the spirit of wisdom and understanding, the spirit of counsel and might, the spirit of knowledge and fear of the Lord.'[3]

Michael Ramsey was concerned because he saw the supernatural,

211

or paranormal activity of the Holy Spirit, being played down too much by the Church and notes that wherever 'the future role of the Christians is formulated, the Spirit is *the* dominant factor in that role'.

Ramsey was therefore concerned enough to stress the need for the Church to have 'an ecclesiology which gives the Spirit a greater place' than much familiar western ecclesiology does. There is, he says, 'a need to remember the continuing lively action of the Spirit whereby alone the believers are Christ's body' and that 'the charismata [charismatic gifts of the Spirit] are constant actions of the Spirit in which the *liveliness* of God *touches* human lives'. Throughout history, he notes, 'the Spirit is invading RUACH *as well as* indwelling PNEUMA'.[4] Sounds much like that distinction between Holy Spirit empowering *and* 'Mr' Holy Spirit that I have explained earlier.

Charles Gore, a great evangelical and first Bishop of Liverpool at the end of the nineteenth century, believed in the need to stress much more than we do the work of the Spirit. It is said that whenever he recited the Creed and said 'I believe in the Holy Catholic Church', he meant by that 'I believe in the Holy Spirit *revivifying* the Church'.

One of the most serious consequences arising from the fear people have of supernatural gifts of the Spirit is that for centuries much of the leadership of the Church have talked people out of any kind of expectation in such realms. So, in confirmation or when praying for the Holy Spirit, the preamble so often is, 'Don't expect anything dramatic or startling to happen' . . . No wonder someone was so exasperated at such minimal levels of expectation as to describe confirmation as 'empty hands on empty heads'! That did not endear him to the archbishops and bishops gathered at that conference in East Africa!

If you find that difficult, Jesus says, then 'believe because of the things I do'.[5]

I have already mentioned how much Jesus' life was steeped in prayer. He had such a close and intimate relationship with His Father in Heaven. So much so that He confidently makes two startling assertions (considering He was also fully man):

(i) He *said* nothing unless God told him to say it:

'. . . I *SAY* only what the Father has instructed Me to say';[6] and 'What, *I say* then, is what the Father has told Me to say'.[7]

(ii) He *did* nothing unless God told Him to do it:

'I am telling you the truth; the Son of Man can *DO* nothing on His own; he *DOES* only what He sees His Father doing';[8] and

'I can *DO* nothing on My own authority; I judge only as God tells Me, so My judgement is right, because I am not trying to do what I want, but only what He who sent Me wants';[9] and yet again,

'I *DO* nothing on My own authority'.[10]

Christ's miracles are proofs of His divine Mission, not only for the conviction of unbelievers, but also for the confirmation of our own faith and those of our fellow believers. Nothing builds up a congregation's faith more than to witness God at work doing 'signs and wonders'.

And Jesus gives us *our* commission: 'As the Father sent Me, so send I you'.[11]

'I am telling you the truth: whoever' [there is a totally all embracing word for doubters] – 'whoever believes in Me will do what I do – yes, he will do even greater things, because I am going to the Father'.[12]

I have heard people explaining the 'greater' things by suggesting it means, or refers to, the sum total of all the signs and wonders from the time of Christ until now. But the context in which it is said doesn't suggest that; however unbelievable (in our human understanding), it is '*whoever*'; it is '*he*' (singular) who will do even greater things! I long simply to do the things Jesus did!

'And I will do whatever you ask for in My name so that *the Father's glory*" [remember the Lord's Prayer?] 'will be shown through the Son. If you ask Me for anything in My name, I will do it.'[13]

It is *not* that God will do anything that I selfishly want Him to do – like give me a super car, triple my income, or whatever. It is for those things which bring glory to the Father; it is for those things that are in accordance with His will. And it includes all the promises we can lay claim to in Scripture.

To Reign or Not to Reign

Our problem is in actually believing it. And not only believing it, but overcoming a bigger hurdle: believing God can use even little insignificant you or me! And the biggest hurdle of all: to move beyond that and actually *act* on it, in *believing* prayer!

Paul the Apostle, and Jesus especially . . . speak of the *power* of the Holy Spirit that is not only available, but is something God longs for all of us to experience! The *power* of the Holy Spirit is so awesome that He, the Holy Spirit, could bring order out of chaos in the formation of the world in Genesis 1:1-3! His power is such that He raised Jesus from death!

And, as Jesus said, this gifting is for "*whoever*"! There are no limitations or conditions attached. One does not have to have special degrees, or hold a special office, or even be licensed or ordained in some special way. Nor does one need any particular formula for this supernatural gifting. As Joel put it, the Spirit will be poured out on anyone *who longs for it*: '. . . your sons and daughters will proclaim My message; your old men will have dreams, and your young men will see visions. At that time I will pour out My Spirit *even on servants [slaves]*, both men and women'.[14]

A number of cartoons appeared over the years, all in much the same vein. A congregation gathered for worship is asked to pray for young Joe Soap who is critically ill in hospital this Sunday morning, and not expected to live. (A shiver runs up the spines of those who know the family well!) The next picture shows Joe Soap walking into church the next Sunday, with the sidesmen commenting in surprise . . . 'We didn't expect to see you again!'

An equally marvellous illustration of that is given to us in the Acts of the Apostles. Peter was imprisoned, guarded by sixteen soldiers, and chained as well. 'The people of the church were praying earnestly to God for him'.[15]

In the light of what was to follow, one has to ask the questions:

i) *What* was the specific thing they were praying for?

and

ii) What did they *expect* as a result of their prayer?

An angel came to Peter's rescue! (In answer to their prayers?):

Peter followed him out of the prison, not knowing, however, if what the angel was doing was real; he thought he was seeing a vision . . . Then Peter realized what had happened to him, and said, 'Now I know that it is really true! The Lord sent His angel to rescue me from Herod's power and from everything the Jewish people expected to happen'.
Aware of his situation, he went to the home of Mary, the mother of John Mark, where many people had gathered and were praying. Peter knocked at the outside door, and a servant-girl named Rhoda came to answer it.[16]

Rhoda was the *only* person in that praying congregation who actually believed their prayer had been answered: 'She recognised Peter's voice and was so happy that she ran back in without opening the door, and announced that Peter was standing outside.'[17]
What about those gathered in the house praying? Judge from their response:
'"You are mad!" they told her. But she insisted that it was true. So they answered, "It is his angel." Meanwhile Peter kept on knocking. At last they opened the door, and when they saw him, they were amazed.'[18]
God continues to interact with his people today. He answers prayer. He delights to see His children made whole spiritually, mentally and physically. He often waits for that 'believing' prayer to come from our hearts. Would it not be true that sometimes we don't receive because we haven't asked, or because we had little or no expectation that anything was possible?
And yes, God continues to *speak* to His people, even though such messages can sometimes be most uncomfortable or cause great anger. Bishop David Pytches, for instance, tells the story of a woman standing in York Minster three days before it was struck by lightning. He vouches for the veracity of the story because he knew this Christian woman personally. She was standing in the transept soon to be gutted by fire.

To Reign or Not to Reign

Like so many others at the time, she marvelled at the wonderful work of restoration that had just been completed in the Minster.

As she looked up at the rose window, she heard a voice speaking to her: 'In three days I will destroy this temple'.

At first she simply dismissed it as a piece of Scripture coming to mind. But the voice repeated it several times. Then slowly it dawned on her that it was not from Scripture, for the text in St John's Gospel says something very different. The actual quotation is: 'Jesus answered them, "Destroy this temple, and I will raise it again in three days".'

That reference spoke of others destroying the Temple, and Christ restoring it! But what this woman was hearing was just the opposite: 'In three days I will destroy this temple'.

It was one of those troubling things, try as she might, she could not dismiss from her mind. For the next three days the words continued to trouble her, but she could think of no logical explanation for them. And then the Minster was struck by lightning, and the roof of that particular transept was destroyed in the ensuing fire. Mercifully the rose window was saved. Later, the woman believed she had been given a prophetic word.

Some, disconcerting as it may be, associate the event with John Habgood, the Archbishop of York's decision to consecrate David Jenkins as Bishop of Durham. He did so *despite* a massive number of written objections on the grounds of Jenkins' heretical statements, and his denials of basic credal beliefs.

Apart from the lightning strike at York, there have been many devastating events in the all too recent past. The sinking of the Herald of Free Enterprise; the Kegworth air crash on the M1; the Lockerbie disaster with a jet liner blown out of the sky at 40,000 feet; the Piper Alpha fireball; a continuing spate of horrifying train crashes; the horrific fireball at King's Cross Tube Station. There were the various mindless massacres of innocent people: those killed in Hungerford by a lone gun freak; all those little children and their teacher shot to death at Dunblane by another mad gunman; a man wielding a machete against nursery children and their heroic young minder in a school playground;

Clinging to a Lamppost at Dawn

the Headteacher Stephen Lawrence knifed to death at the gates of his school; the senseless battering to death of baby Jamie Bulger by two teenagers.

Other catastrophes incude Liverpool's Hillsborough football disaster; the appalling devastation wreaked by hurricanes in the affluent south east; the stock exchange crash three days after one of those hurricanes.

In addition we see continuing street violence, youngsters out of control, massive increases in thefts and burglaries, particularly by juveniles, and deaths and mayhem caused by 'joy' riding, and road rage. There was Black (or White?) Wednesday – depending on your point of view.

There is the pain, turmoil and disintegration of society: the massive unemployment, scandal of house repossessions, and negative equity problems in the 80s and 90s. Increasing violence, rapes, battering, ram raiding, mugging, murdering of the elderly, often for no more than a few pence, to provide money for drugs. There is, and has been, the infamy of child abuse on a massive scale, and by no means restricted to Children's Homes in Wales; the murder of two-million-plus unborn babies (Psalm 139:13); increasing pornography, sexual aberration, with anything goes on TV channels after 9 p.m. and sometimes before!

There is the growing scale of drunkenness and sexual promiscuity in school children, permissiveness in society generally, and the breakdown of family life and advocating of single parent families; the senseless and frightening escalation in sectarian bombing and killings; the industrial decay, and boarded-up shops and businesses; the hopeless and growing poverty and despair for many – while the rich get richer, with massive and totally immoral salaries and perks paid to the 'privileged'; and mammoth frauds in big business; the scandal of the money markets and mis-selling . . .

Would it be surprising that more and more prophecies are received that 'speak' to us in our situation? Do we have the ears to hear what the Spirit is saying to the Church, and the nation?

The Lord Almighty has a controversy with this nation . . . for years you have sown the wind and you are beginning to reap the whirlwind . . . I am handing you over to your own wilful ways; I am taking My hands of protection from you. I will no longer look upon you with favour and you will be overtaken by your own wickedness *unless* you repent and turn to Me . . .'

The Lord says to . . . the shepherds . . . I have called you to feed and guard my sheep . . . but you have fed them with junk food . . . you are so blinded by your own unbelief. You . . . are spiritually sick because you do not believe the truth of My Word. You have substituted for it the teachings of men and the empty thoughts of your minds. Why do you cause my people to doubt the truth of what I have said? It is because of you that the churches are empty and the faithful few so weak and powerless and despairing. Who will come to the place of feeding when they receive garbage instead of bread? I call to you to repent of your unbelief before it is too late. If you will not, know that I will not overlook your sin . . . do not think that such a day of reckoning is far off . . . In My love and grief and deep concern, I call to you now before it is too late . . .

My people, what have you done with My Spirit? I sent Him to lead you back into ways of holiness, but you have continued to turn a blind eye to sin . . . and substitute renewal for repentance. How can you so fly in the face of all He [the Spirit] wanted to do? You have been breaking My heart and put Me to shame in the face of the world, but you have not cared. I wanted to send repentance and revival so as to touch a lost world for which My heart aches, but you have prevented Me. You have used My Holy Spirit for your own ends . . . You have made Me grieve . . . weep . . . Will you not now repent and turn to the ways I have chosen for you?

And God continues to call to all who truly love Him: 'I look to you

My people, to honour My name in the midst of an unbelieving people.'[20]

It's so easy isn't it, something the devil majors on, to find our lives governed by 'if only's', by regrets, by so many negative thoughts and attitudes?

My concern was that I might be 'over the hill' or had outlived my usefulness. Sometimes we do nothing, or refuse to speak up because we think there is little that someone as insignificant as you or me can do to change our church, community or nation for the better.

Whatever has marked the pattern of one's life or experience of God, it is never too late to begin a new move with God. And why shouldn't we be bold enough to move into realms and dimensions never experienced before? Here is a challenge. If we fail to take it up, we will be the losers. What could not God do with a person who is fully submitted to Him?

Let me tell you what little I know of Daphne's story. I met her at a Healing Centre in Bournemouth where I was conducting a week's conference. What immediately struck me about her was how tired and frail she looked. I am not sure of her age, but I thought it would be about four score years! She had loved the Lord all her life, and served Him faithfully. When she came to ask for prayer, she told us of her love for Jesus, but explained that suddenly she seemed to have lost a little of her joy and hope. And not surprisingly!

A year previously her husband of many, many happy and fruitful years of partnership had died. Shortly afterwards one of those hurricanes that hit the south east struck their large home. She was in bed asleep at the time. She had a miraculous escape, because the outside wall of the room she was in just fell away! All the problems of getting it rebuilt, put back to rights, and dealing with the insurers – on top of looking after a large property – were just beyond her. Kind friends advised her to sell and move out.

This is a trauma in anyone's life, especially when it has been your home for most of a lifetime. Her friends also advised her to move into a block of flats for security.

It was quite a way from where she had lived previously, and a quite different sort of neighbourhood. She could no longer get to the church where she had been so happy. She was too far away from the friends she had lived amongst to see them more than infrequently. She had lost her garden and felt marooned within her flat. And the worst scenario – the flats turned out to be not in the best of neighbourhoods. Many who lived in them were fearful of going out unaccompanied. Some of the youngsters were pretty wild, and the new church to which she went was just not the same!

But what was so remarkable about this story was that Daphne wasn't actually complaining. Her love for the Lord still shone through it all. Her concern was this: was there nothing more she could do in serving the Lord as she had done previously? Did she just have to accept that she had arrived at that stage in life where God wanted her to put her feet up?

She didn't believe in her heart of hearts that that was right! So she had come to the Conference seeking what the Lord might have for her.

As we prayed for her one evening I shared with her something I believed God wanted her to know; that He was giving her an intercessory ministry for those who lived in her new area, and particularly for the unruly element – those who really needed to know God's love. And although she would often not know what to pray for, or how to pray, the Spirit would pray through her.

It was then that she revealed her real heartache. For years she had longed for the gift of tongues, but never received it. So we prayed, reminding the Lord of His promised new ministry for Daphne, and of her need for this gift of tongues. Nothing seemed to happen, but I encouraged her to believe that God was going to give her that gift, and His timing for it would be right. Just don't get anxious about it, I told her. Just keep praising the Lord as if you had already received it.

A couple of mornings later I was going out for my early morning walk on the beach. Several people had heard about this habit and used to join me. Others just groaned at the thought of being on the beach at 5 a.m.! But on this particular morning as I left my room, I happened to notice a piece of paper stuck under the door of the next room. Knowing

Clinging to a Lamppost at Dawn

it was unoccupied, I picked it up and found the note was addressed to me – from Daphne. She would love to go to the beach! She had not been able to sleep. Was it just possible that this once I could take my car so she could come because she couldn't walk that far? And if that were possible, would I just let her sit in the car at the seafront? So I fetched her from her room and, with several others, went down to the beach. We left her sitting there as we walked off along the water's edge towards Poole harbour.

Let Daphne tell you what happened next.

'As the sun came over the horizon, it was so beautiful that I got out and wandered on to the foreshore. And then it happened. I felt myself being bathed in love, literally swamping me with a wonderful sense of warmth. And then I was speaking in this strange language, in tongues, and I just didn't want to stop. I had to stagger to the nearest lamppost for support.

'At that moment a security guard drove down the path alongside the beach. He couldn't believe he was seeing a drunken octogenerian weaving across the path and then clinging to this lamppost. He stopped his car and came across to ask if I needed help.

'When he got to me, I asked, "Do you know Jesus?" He replied in the affirmative. He was a good practising Christian and a member of a lively Fellowship! I explained about attending the conference, the prayers I had received, and how right here on the beach Jesus had baptized me with His Spirit in answer to our prayers. And so together we praised God!

'When he had to move on, he was concerned about leaving me there. But I assured him I was with others – perhaps he had seen them as he came up from the Poole Harbour end? I described the group, including our pastor who was wearing shorts! He told me he had seen the group a couple of miles back. I told him he didn't have to wait. I would just stay where I was, holding on to my lamppost, and continue to use this beautiful new language God had given me'.

As we came down the beach again some while later, I was amazed

To Reign or Not to Reign

to see Daphne staggering across the sand towards me, crying with joy as she kept repeating . . . 'John, isn't it wonderful! God has answered my prayer. I can speak in tongues' and just threw herself into my arms.

As she left in her taxi the next morning there was such a joy bubbling out of her. The tiredness and frailty seemed to have been swept away. As she said, 'God has not only given me a new job to do, but He has equipped me for it with His own marvellous gift!'

Like Rolf she could just as easily have said, 'Not retired, re-fired!'

I will always remember Daphne with a special sense of wonder at God's miraculous activity. Clinging to her lamppost on the beachfront … at dawn. Drunk with God's Spirit. Leaving the Conference with a positive sense of purpose at God's latest call and equipping that would, who knows, enable her to do great exploits for God in her new environment.

What could not God do with a person who is fully submitted to Him?

I the Lord of sea and sky,
I have heard My people cry . . .
Who will bear My light to them?
Whom shall I send?
>*Here I am, Lord,*
>*Is it I, Lord,*
>*I have heard you calling in the night.*
>*I will go, Lord,*
>*If you lead me;*
>*I will hold your people in my heart.*[21]

NOTES:
[1] Acts 2:13,15
[2] *Holy Spirit* Michael Ramsey (SPCK 1977)
Bible references: See Micah 3:8, Isaiah 42:1,
Ezekiel 11:19,20,36:24–27 and 37:4–6,10
[3] Isa. 11:1–3 (RSV); cf Isa 61:1–2 and Joel 2:28–29
[4] ibid.

Clinging to a Lamppost at Dawn

[5] John 14:11b
[6] John 8:28b
[7] John 12:50b
[8] John 5:19
[9] John 5:30
[10] John 8:28
[11] John 20:21
[12] John 4:12
[13] John 14:13,14
[14] Joel 2:28–29
[15] Acts 12:5
[16] Acts 12:9,11–13
[17] Acts 12:14
[18] Acts 12:15–16
[19] John 2:19 (*RSV*)
[20] Selections of prophecies recorded at recent Conferences.
[21] 'I the Lord of sea and sky' copyright 1981 Daniel L. Schutte and New Dawn Music

Epilogue

SWEET SPIRIT

Ruach, Ruach, Wind of the Spirit,
Wind of the Spirit flow into me.
Fill me anew with Your love and power;
loving me; strengthening me; enabling me
to do *all* that my Lord would have me do.

Grant me, sweet Spirit,
the gifts that I need,
to fulfil the tasks
of my Father's design,
and grow in me daily
Your precious fruit,
so with Jesus alone
my life may shine.

26.1.93   Diana Wilkinson

To Reign or Not to Reign

RUACH – WIND OF THE SPIRIT

Ruach! Breath!
Wind of the Spirit:
Breath of the Living God
breathe Your life-giving Breath
on me.
Fill me, O Lord,
that I may be
what You would have me be
and do
what You would have me do.

Spirit of God descend I pray
on this church of ours:
fill its people with such great hunger
for You
that we'll pray without ceasing
till we're filled anew,
as at Pentecost
all those years ago

Pentecost power was no gentle infilling,
no quiet Spirit within –
the thing that we have

Epilogue

from the time of our baptism,
or giving our lives to God –
but a coming in rushing mighty wind;
in tongues of flame and fire
that changed the lives of timid people
into valiant warriors for God:
into people *empowered*
– and able to *do*
the things that Christ had done.

What do you want,
my friends, my brothers and sisters?
– to sit in a cosy pew,
worshipping God respectably,
calmly, safely?
or do you want to witness anew
the *power* of the Living Christ today,
at work in your life and mine?

Do you want to be used,
in a powerful way,
to bring His Kingdom in;
to see His world, His people
saved?
Do you want to witness the lame leap,
enable the blind to see
and make broken lives whole?

'I'll send you My Spirit,'
Jesus said,
'and these things, and greater,
you'll do.'
'Go, wait for the Spirit to come
and *then empowered* go out.'

To Reign or Not to Reign

Not in our strength, dear friends,
can we do it,
but only by the *Power of His Spirit*,
and that we'll receive if we ask Him,
but only if we hunger and thirst,
and go on and on asking
without ceasing.

In His word it says,
'Ask and you'll receive,
seek and you *will* find –
but the Greek words mean
'ask and go on and on and on
asking and seeking.'
We are commanded to seek
and *persist* in that seeking,
until that same Pentecost power
is *ours*,
and *then* the Spirit of God will come,
and not just quietly dwell within,
but *flow through*,
to be *used* by me and you
that the world may know
God is God;
Jesus is Lord,
the same yesterday, today and tomorrow.
Power Divine –
to heal and save.

Will *we* really go on asking?
Do we really want to see
the *power* of God at work today,
manifest through you and me?
Do we want to witness God's glory?

Epilogue

If so, pray.
Ask the Holy Spirit of God
to come:
seek His gifts
and be willing to use them,
for Him,
today
and every day.

PENTECOST, 1992.   Diana Wilkinson

(Both poems used with permission. The latter poem Diana wrote during the Pentecost weekend of 1992. I was conducting a Holy Spirit Conference in Bournemouth that week-end, and Diana shared it with those present at the time. The first poem was written a year later and sent to me by Diana.)